I NEVER KNEW THAT
ABOUT BRITAIN
THE QUIZ BOOK

I Never Knew That About England
I Never Knew That About Ireland
I Never Knew That About Scotland
I Never Knew That About Wales
I Never Knew That About London
I Never Knew That About the English
I Never Knew That About the Irish
I Never Knew That About the Scottish

CHRISTOPHER WINN

I NEVER KNEW THAT
ABOUT BRITAIN
THE QUIZ BOOK

ILLUSTRATIONS BY
Mai Osawa

EBURY
PRESS

For Hyla, Jane and the boys –
the ultimate quizmasters

7 9 10 8

Published in 2009 by Ebury Press, an imprint of Ebury Publishing

A Random House Group Company

Text © Christopher Winn 2009
Illustrations © Mai Osawa 2009

The Random House Group Limited Reg. No. 954009

Addresses for companies within the Random House Group
can be found at www.randomhouse.co.uk

A CIP catalogue record for this book is available from the British Library

To buy books by your favourite authors and register for offers
visit www.randomhouse.co.uk

Series design by Peter Ward
Typeset by Palimpsest Book Production Limited,
Grangemouth, Stirlingshire
Printed and bound by CPI Group (UK) Ltd, Croydon, CR0 4YY

ISBN: 9780091933043

CONTENTS

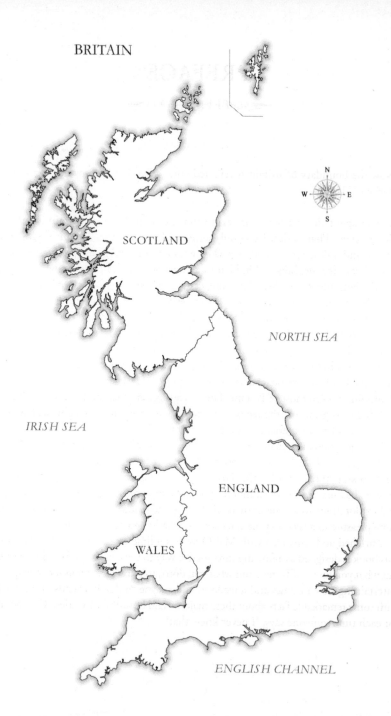

BRITAIN

SCOTLAND

NORTH SEA

IRISH SEA

ENGLAND

WALES

ENGLISH CHANNEL

PREFACE

'Now the boundary of Britain is revealed and everything unknown is held to be glorious.' Tacitus

Having spent the last few years exploring the boundaries of Britain for the 'I Never Knew That' series, I can only agree with Tacitus that Britain is glorious, known and unknown – a land so packed with treasure and beauty, so blessed with blissful countryside, hills and hidden valleys, woods and waters, so enhanced with breathtaking and venerable architecture, castles, cathedrals, village churches, palaces, stately mansions, homely cottages of stone and wood, ingenious bridges and tunnels and innovations. Britain is vibrant and alive with the tales and poetry of heroes and lovers and scoundrels, of battles and of peace, of kings and queens, achievements and dreams, every kind of human drama and character.

There is still so much to see and absorb, so many surprises to make one gasp and shake the head with disbelief and wonder and joy, that I cannot claim to know all of Britain, or even most of Britain. There is always so much more of it to discover and that is its great joy; the realisation that it will never fail to delight, will always be a source of new experiences and excitements.

This quiz book is a chance to sum up and revisit what I have learned of Britain so far. I have collected so much knowledge and already forgotten so much, there is need to stop and take a breath. Deciding on the questions and researching the answers has allowed me to summon up many happy memories of pleasurable trips and explorations to all the corners of these islands, and I hope you will find the same pleasure in answering the questions as I had in compiling them.

Enriched and enhanced with Mai Osawa's sublime and evocative illustrations, this book is designed as a fun and informative way to travel through Britain, to find out what you know of Britain and what you don't, to refresh the memory, to acquire entertaining new insights and anecdotes and maybe to dazzle friends and family with some remarkable facts about these majestic and beautiful countries. One point for each time someone says, 'I never knew that!'.

GENERAL KNOWLEDGE

'Knowledge is power.'
FRANCIS BACON

'A little knowledge is a dangerous thing.'

1) What is Britain's newest national park?

2) What kind of tree is sometimes known as a May tree?

3) Which Scottish king was born in Turnberry, Ayrshire, or Lochmaben, Dumfriesshire – or possibly Writtle in Essex?

4) Which river does the longest railway tunnel wholly within Britain pass under?

5) A species of what kind of bird takes its name from Northumberland-born illustrator and wood engraver Thomas Bewick?

6) In what county town did Marconi set up the world's first radio factory?

7) What language was Dolly Pentreath, who died in 1777, the last person known to have spoken?

8) What is the only English county name to contain five consonants in a row?

9) On what island is Holyhead?

10) Where in Scotland is it said to be so windy that 'when the wind drops everyone falls over'?

'If a little knowledge is dangerous – where is the man who has so much as to be out of danger?'

THOMAS HUXLEY

1) What is the most westerly cathedral city in Britain?

2) What is unique about British stamps?

3) Who painted a portrait of Winston Churchill which, according to Churchill himself, made him look as if he was 'straining a stool'?

4) What is the county town of Merioneth?

5) Which television situation comedy was filmed at the manor house in Cricket St Thomas in Somerset?

6) Which fishing port, site of Scotland's first lighthouse, was founded by Sir Alexander Fraser in 1546?

7) Which home was built for the first Briton to rise from a commoner to a Duke in one generation?

8) On which river does Canterbury stand?

9) Who wrote his seminal work while living at his mother's house in Kirkcaldy in Fife and observing workers at the local nail factory?

10) What was the first British car to sell a million?

'There is much pleasure to be gained from useless knowledge.'

BERTRAND RUSSELL

1) Hereford claims to be the birthplace of which of Charles II's mistresses?

2) What is the highest village in Scotland? BONUS QUESTION: And the second highest?

3) Name the English castle where Richard III was born in 1452 and where Mary, Queen of Scots, was beheaded in 1587?

4) In what town is the Shepherd Neame brewery, the oldest brewery in England?

5) What make of car was the 'Old Speckled 'Un', which was built in 1927 and which gave its name to a beer brewed originally in Abingdon, Berkshire?

6) Who designed the Willow Tea Room in Glasgow?

7) Which town do world motor racing champion Lewis Hamilton and thriller writer Ken Follett's wife Barbara have in common?

8) Which is Britain's busiest railway station, in terms of trains passing through?

9) Which Scottish county boasts of the Rhins and the Machars?

10) Until the Industrial Revolution what was the largest town in Wales?

'Try to know everything of something,
and something of everything.'

LORD BROUGHAM

1) How was Ursula Sontheil, born in a cave near Knaresborough in 1488, better known?

2) Which cathedral was destroyed by the Wolf of Badenoch?

3) What did William Hillman make in Coventry before he made cars?

4) Which early English philosopher influenced the American Revolution with his philosophy, 'The ruling body, if it offends against natural law, must be deposed'?

5) How many letters are there in the following name? Llanfairpwllgwyngyllgogerychwy rndrobwllllantysiliogogogoch

6) Where did the British Cabinet meet for the first time ever outside London, in 1921?

7) What county is known as the 'county of spires and squires'?

8) Which Welsh castle has the thickest castle walls in the world?

9) Which king led the English to victory at the Battle of Agincourt in 1415?

10) What drink, 'made in Scotland from girders', was carted around Falkirk in Stirlingshire in the 1930s by Carnera, 'the biggest horse in the world'?

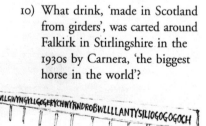

LLANFAIRPWLLGWYNGYLLGOGERYCHWYRNDROBWLLLLANTYSILIOGOGOGOCH

'One cannot know everything.'

HORACE

1) The capital of the US State of Connecticut takes its name from the county town of which British county?

2) What is the most northerly town in the world located on the Prime Meridian?

3) Which Scottish family name comes from the Gaelic for 'crooked mouth'? BONUS QUESTION: And 'crooked nose'?

4) Which English county is most associated with well dressing?

5) There are only three cable-hauled street tramways in the world, in San Francisco, Lisbon and which Welsh town?

6) Which legendary highwayman lived as a Yorkshire gentleman called John Palmer?

7) Which cathedral contains the highest bishop's chair in Christendom?

8) Harry Corbett was nephew to Harry Ramsden, founder of the world's largest fish and chip shop, and played the piano there – what was the name of his puppet?

9) Who has the same name as a new Scottish city and founded the SAS?

10) Ogof Ffynnon Ddu, which at 1,010 ft (308 m) in depth is Britain's deepest cave, can be found in which national park?

'Pocket all your knowledge with your watch and never pull it out in company unless desired.'

LORD CHESTERFIELD

1) Which writer had an unhappy affair with the philosopher Herbert Spencer?

2) What breed of dog was Greyfriars Bobby?

3) What surname is shared by the man who described Oxford as the 'city of dreaming spires' and the first English composer to win an Oscar, for the score for *Bridge on the River Kwai*, in 1957?

4) Which Welsh port has the longest breakwater in Britain?

5) Which comedian was born John Eric Bartholomew and later changed his name to that of the town where he was born in 1926?

6) Which iconic British car went on sale in 1959 for £500?

7) In which year did Red Rum, the most successful horse in the history of the race, achieve the first of his three Grand National victories?

8) Which Queen sank in Hong Kong Harbour in 1975?

9) Which county produces over half of England's cider?

10) Auchinleck House in Ayrshire is the ancestral home of which 18th-century writer?

'All men by nature desire to know.'

ARISTOTLE

1) In which British city would you be if you were walking down the Shambles?

2) What name is given to the area a team of oxen can comfortably plough in one morning?

3) Black Bart, born in Pembrokeshire in 1682, was the first pirate known to have flown what?

4) Where would you go to walk along the longest seaside pier in the world?

5) What is Scotland's National Book Town?

6) What is the most common adjective in the *Oxford English Dictionary*?

7) Name Scotland's two Formula One world champions.

8) What is the name of the bell that hangs in the Lloyds underwriting room and used to be rung to announce news of overdue ships – once for bad news and twice for good news?

9) What brand design includes the phrase from the Book of Judges 'out of the strong came forth sweetness', and is the oldest unchanged brand design in Britain?

10) In which county would you find the A5114, at less than 2 miles (3 km) long Britain's shortest A road?

'I am not young enough to know everything.'

Oscar Wilde

1) On what island is Talisker whisky made?

2) Which industrial giant grew out of the Cheshire salt mines?

3) What was the first make of car to be manufactured at Longbridge in Birmingham?

4) Which county does the biggest breed of terrier, the Airedale, hail from?

5) Which well-preserved 18th-century ironworks in Monmouthshire is now a World Heritage Site?

6) What was the most popular name for a king of Scotland before the Stewarts?

7) Which Welsh county is the most scarcely populated and has the lowest levels of light pollution in England or Wales?

8) Where did the German High Seas Fleet scuttle itself in 1919?

9) Will Adams, born in Gillingham in 1564, was the first Englishman to reach which country?

10) How many English kings have been called Edward?

Multiple choice

1) Frederick, Prince of Wales, who expired in 1751, was the first man to die as a result of being hit with what?
a) A cricket ball
b) A sandwich
c) A car

2) 'It is not for glory, nor riches, nor honours that we are fighting, but for freedom . . .' Where do these words come from?
a) Magna Carta
b) American Declaration of Independence
c) Declaration of Arbroath

3) Who was the first agricultural labourer to become an MP?
a) John Prescott
b) Joseph Arch
c) George Loveless

4) Which Archbishop of Canterbury negotiated Magna Carta with King John?
a) Thomas à Becket
b) Thomas More
c) Stephen Langton

5) What did Kirkpatrick Macmillan invent at his smithy in the hills of Dumfriesshire?
a) Printing press
b) Monkey wrench
c) Pedal bicycle

6) What is the oldest surviving folk festival in England?
a) Abbots Bromley Horn Dance
b) Padstow Hobby Horse
c) Olney Pancake Race

7) What is the only town that stands right on Offa's Dyke?
a) Oswestry
b) Knighton
c) Ludlow

8) What is the most commonly used letter in the English language?
a) E
b) S
c) O

9) Who went over to New York to collect Thomas Paine's bones and bring them back to be buried in Thetford in Norfolk, Paine's birthplace, only to lose them?
a) Daniel Defoe
b) William Cobbett
c) Dylan Thomas

10) What was the seat of Scotland's first bishopric, in the 7th century?
a) Iona
b) Aberdeen
c) Abercorn

11) What dockyard was the largest operational flying-boat base in the world during the Second World War?
a) Portsmouth
b) Dundee
c) Pembroke Dock

12) What did William Morris describe as 'the supremest specimen of all ugliness'?
a) St Pancras Station
b) Forth Railway Bridge
c) Truro Cathedral

13) What is Scotland's most northerly Munro?
a) Ben Hope
b) Ben Nevis
c) Ben Lomond

14) What body of water does John Ruskin's home, Brantwood, overlook?
a) Loch Lomond
b) Lake Vyrnwy
c) Coniston Water

15) What did Elizabeth I's godson Sir John Harington invent?
a) Gunpowder
b) Water closet
c) Ink

16) Who could claim that both grandfathers were members of the Lunar Society?
a) William Fox-Talbot
b) Aldous Huxley
c) Charles Darwin

17) What is the largest medieval gothic cathedral in England?
a) Lincoln
b) York Minster
c) Salisbury

18) Who coined the phrase 'corridors of power'?
a) Edmund Burke
b) George Orwell
c) C.P. Snow

19) James IV was the last Scottish king to die in battle. At which battle did he die?
a) Culloden
b) Prestonpans
c) Flodden

20) What is the Boston Stump?
a) A tree
b) A church tower
c) A boat

Odd one out

1) Which of these writers did NOT graduate from Oxford University?
a) Oscar Wilde
b) Anthony Powell
c) Graham Greene
d) Sir John Betjeman

2) Which of these was NOT invented by a Scotsman?
a) Pneumatic tyre
b) Steam turbine
c) Adhesive postage stamp
d) Hypnosis

3) Which of these hymns was NOT written by an Englishman?
a) 'Once in Royal David's City'
b) 'Amazing Grace'
c) 'Jerusalem'
d) 'Rock of Ages'

4) Which of these was NOT the home of a prime minister?
a) Cliveden House
b) Hawarden Castle
c) Dalmeny House
d) Hughenden Manor

5) Which of these was NOT founded by Quakers?
a) Cadbury's
b) Lloyds Bank
c) Bryant and May
d) Lloyds Insurance

6) Which of these was NOT designed by a Scott?
a) Red telephone box
b) Albert Memorial
c) Guildford Cathedral
d) Shakespeare Memorial Theatre, Stratford

7) Which of these was NOT Poet Laureate?
a) Ben Jonson
b) Sir Walter Scott
c) Ted Hughes
d) Alfred, Lord Tennyson

8) Which of the following was NOT born in Bedfordshire?
a) John Bunyan
b) Margaret Beaufort
c) Sir Joseph Paxton
d) Ralph Vaughan Williams

9) Which of these members of the Bloomsbury Group is NOT buried in Sussex?
a) Virginia Woolf
b) Duncan Grant
c) Vanessa Bell
d) Lytton Strachey

10) Which of these musical acts which reached No. 1 in the charts is NOT from Liverpool?
a) Atomic Kitten
b) Frankie Goes to Hollywood
c) Oasis
d) Dead or Alive

11) Which of these monarchs is NOT buried in St George's Chapel, Windsor?
a) Queen Victoria
b) Henry VIII
c) Charles I
d) George III

12) Which of these is NOT a county town?
a) Colchester
b) Dorchester
c) Oakham
d) Reading

13) Which of these cathedrals does NOT have a central tower?
a) Canterbury
b) Exeter
c) Worcester
d) Gloucester

14) Which of these is NOT a highest point?
a) Cleeve Hill – 1,083 ft (330 m)
b) Scafell Pike – 3,209 ft (978 m)
c) Herefordshire Beacon – 1,109 ft (338 m)
d) Brown Willy – 1,378 ft (420 m)

15) Which of these is NOT a spa town?
a) Ashbourne, Derbyshire
b) Cheltenham, Gloucestershire
c) Malvern, Worcestershire
d) Epsom, Surrey

16) Which of these writers was NOT born in Edinburgh (right)?
a) Neil Munro
b) Sir Walter Scott
c) Robert Louis Stevenson
d) Sir Arthur Conan Doyle

17) Which of these banks was NOT started by a Scotsman?
a) Barclays
b) HSBC
c) Coutts
d) Co-operative Bank

18) Which of these mountains is NOT a Munro?
a) Lochnagar
b) Ben Hope
c) The Merrick
d) Ben Macdhui

19) Which of these towns is NOT a county town?
a) Dingwall
b) Dornoch
c) Berwick-on-Tweed
d) Jedburgh

20) Which of these buildings is NOT designed by an Adam?
a) Culzean Castle
b) Duff House
c) Paxton House
d) Kinross House

21) Which of these is definitely NOT buried in St David's Cathedral?
a) Giraldus Cambrensis
b) Henry Tudor
c) St David
d) Rhys Ap Gruffudd

22) Which of these kings was NOT born in Wales?
a) Henry VII
b) Edward III
c) Edward II
d) Henry V

23) Which of these mountains is NOT in Wales?
a) Pen-y-Fan
b) Mount Snowdon
c) Helvellyn
d) Moel Famau

24) Which of these towns is NOT a county town?
a) Montgomery
b) Machynlleth
c) Beaumaris
d) Presteigne

25) Which of these politicians was NOT born in Wales?
a) Geoffrey Howe
b) Michael Heseltine
c) John Prescott
d) William Gladstone

26) Which of these monarchs was NOT crowned at Westminster Abbey?
a) William the Conqueror
b) Elizabeth I
c) Edward VIII
d) Henry II

27) Which of these towns does NOT lie on the River Great Ouse?
a) Bedford
b) Peterborough
c) Huntingdon
d) Ely

28) Which one of these is NOT among the original Cinque Ports?
a) Hastings
b) Dover
c) Rye
d) Sandwich

29) Which of these Prime Ministers was NOT educated at Harrow?
a) Spencer Perceval
b) Winston Churchill
c) Pandit Nehru
d) William Gladstone

30) Which of these racing drivers was NOT Formula One world champion?
a) Stirling Moss
b) Lewis Hamilton
c) Damon Hill
d) James Hunt

Can you find the one and only?

1) Britain's only rack-and-pinion railway climbs what mountain?

2) Name England's only cape.

3) Which is the only British regiment to take its name from a town?

4) What is the only body of water in the Lake District to have the word 'lake' in its name?

5) Which clergyman, born in East Lothian, was the only active clergyman to sign the American Declaration of Independence?

6) Which English artist's birthplace is the only one in Britain open to the public?

7) Which is the only traditional Welsh county to span Wales from east to west?

8) Which was the only British city to have its medieval cathedral destroyed by bombing during the Second World War?

9) Prestwick airport was the only place in Britain where who set foot?

10) Who is Britain's only native-born national saint?

11) Which is the only English cathedral to have three spires?

12) Who is the only person in Britain to be allowed to keep a private army? BONUS QUESTION: And who gave him permission?

13) Outside which Welsh town would you find the only remaining tinplate works in Britain?

14) Who was the only British person ever to be the editor of a national newspaper and a cabinet minister?

15) Glenelg is Scotland's only what?

16) What is the only English county with two separate coastlines?

17) Who was the only official cardinal the Scots ever had?

18) What is unique about the Orchardton tower house in Kirkcudbrightshire?

19) What is the only English town north of the River Tweed?

20) Where in Wales is the only courthouse in Britain where the jury sits higher than the judge?

21) In which county would you find Scotland's only triangular castle?

22) In which English town would you find the only triangular church tower in Britain?

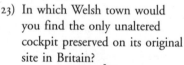

23) In which Welsh town would you find the only unaltered cockpit preserved on its original site in Britain?

24) What English village can boast a church with Britain's only 'Rhenish Helm'?

25) Britain's only remaining fortified bridge stands guard at the entrance to which town?

There's more than one?

1) Where would you find the 4 round churches in England?

2) Name the 7 kingdoms of the Saxon heptarchy.

3) Name 2 Englishmen who have had a Cuban cigar size named after them.

4) Name the 5 official Welsh cities.

5) Which 2 towns claim to have the widest high street in England?

6) Name the 6 Stuart monarchs who sat on the throne of England.

7) Which 2 towns claim to be the highest town in England?

8) In which 3 cities would you find Scotland's 3 crown spires?

9) Where would you find the 4 bridge chapels, actually on their bridge, in England?

10) Where would you find Scotland's 2 round towers?

Which British county do you associate with the following?

1) A sauce, a sausage, a pie and a butcher Duke?

2) Bed time, Europe's oldest open zoo, the Pilgrim's Progress and the RSPB?

3) Pasties, cream, tin, a Lizard, a hobby horse and King Arthur?

4) Corgis, Henry VII, Britain's smallest cathedral city and the Duke of Monmouth's mother?

5) A white rose, a pudding and the biggest expanse of medieval glass in the world?

6) Cheese, a smiling cat, rows of shopping and *Cranford*?

7) Royal and Ancient, the first Carnegie library, *Robinson Crusoe*, Britain's oldest tennis court and *The Wealth of Nations*?

8) Oliver Cromwell, Stilton cheese, John Major and a low point?

9) The birth of evolution, the Industrial Revolution and the modern Olympics, A.E. Housman and the Wrekin?

10) Whale-backed downs, hammer ponds, the only cathedral spire that can be seen from the sea and 1066?

Which British town or city do you associate with the following?

1) Cream sherry, ship shape, the Plimsoll line, the Cabot brothers and the oldest continuously working theatre in Britain?

2) A marmalade, a car, a style of trousers, brogues, a dictionary and the world's first public museum?

3) Golden Shred, the Cradle of the Stewarts, St Mirren football club, a pattern and a shawl?

4) Mustard, insurance, and the Canaries?

5) Gin, the Hoe, Brethren and the Mayflower Steps?

6) The biggest biscuit factory in the world, Henry I's burial place, the Royals, Oscar Wilde?

7) Marmalade, fruit cake, the Beano and Annie Maloney's bell?

8) The world's oldest passenger railway station, the first Rolls-Royce, the *Guardian* and the Hallé Orchestra?

9) Copperopolis, Dylan Thomas's 'ugly, lovely town', a new-born Beau Nash, and the 104th Archbishop of Canterbury?

10) Hobson's Choice, the 'most beautiful mile in the world', a round church and Oliver Cromwell's head?

Do you know what these acronyms stand for?

1) ODEON

2) DVLA

3) TVR

4) TIP

5) HMV

6) MG

7) ICI

8) MCC

9) BBC

10) OBE

Well, I Never Knew This!

The name TESCO is derived from the first two letters of founder Jack Cohen's surname (CO) and the first three letters of his first supplier of tea, T.E. Stockwell (TES).

'Names are not always what they seem. The common Welsh name BZJXXLLWCP is pronounced Jackson.'

MARK TWAIN

1) Who was known as the Lady of the Lamp?

2) The name of which royal house means 'house of steel'?

3) What was the Elephant Man's real name?

4) What is the family name of the Marquess of Ailsa?

5) Who is known as the Big Yin?

6) Which Scottish town is known as Queen of the South?

7) What did the Saxe-Coburg-Gotha family change their name to during the First World War?

8) How were the Knights of St Francis of Wycombe better known?

9) Who was the Immortal Tinker?

10) What city is sometimes known as 'Auld Reekie'?

Well, I Never Knew This!

Sir George Everest, the Surveyor-General of India after whom the world's highest mountain is named, pronounced his name Eve-rest NOT Ever-rest.

Do you know who – real or imagined – said the following?

(Questions 5 and 10 are conversations – name both participants)

1) 'I see my birds have flown.'

2) 'I really do not see the signal.'

3) 'What is our task? To make Britain a fit country for heroes to live in.'

4) 'Vodka Martini – shaken, not stirred'

5) 'By God, Sir, I've lost my leg!'
   'By God, Sir, so you have!'

6) 'An author who speaks about his own books is almost as bad as a mother who talks about her own children.'

7) 'Am in Market Harborough – where should I be?'

8) '. . . when you have eliminated the impossible, whatever remains, however improbable, must be the truth.'

9) 'Patriotism is the last refuge of a scoundrel.'

10) 'Sir, if you were my husband, I would put poison in your tea.'
    'If I were your husband I would drink it.'

Complete the following quotes.
For bonus points, name their author.

1) If I have seen further than others, it is because I was . . . (6 words)

2) Being attacked by Geoffrey Howe is like being . . . (5 words)

3) No man is an island . . . (3 words)

4) Early to bed and early to rise . . . (7 words)

5) When two Englishmen meet, their first talk . . . (4 words)

6) For the female of the species is . . . (5 words)

7) There is only one thing worse than being talked about . . . (7 words)

8) For fools rush in . . . (5 words)

9) Oh what a tangled web we weave . . . (6 words)

10) The people never give up their liberties but . . . (3 words)

GEOGRAPHY

'As a young man, my fondest dream was to become a geographer. However, while working in the customs office I thought deeply about the matter and concluded it was too difficult a subject. With some reluctance I then turned to physics as a substitute.'

ALBERT EINSTEIN

'One sees great things from the valley, only small things from the peak.'

G.K. CHESTERTON

1) What is the highest point in Britain?

2) What is the highest point in Wales?

3) What is the highest point in England?

4) What is the northernmost inhabited island of the British Isles?

5) What is the most northerly point of mainland Britain?

6) What is the most northerly town on mainland Britain?

7) Which estuary is overlooked by the Point of Ayr, the most northerly point of mainland Wales?

8) What is the most easterly point of mainland Britain?

9) What is the most easterly town in Wales?

10) What is the most easterly point of mainland Scotland?

Well, I Never Knew This!

Great Britain is the ninth largest island in the world (discounting Australia, which is a continent).

'He was my North, my South, my East and West . . .'

W.H. Auden

1) Which is furthest east – Orkney or Shetland?

2) Which island is further south – Jersey or Tresco?

3) What is the most southerly point on mainland Britain?

4) What is the most southerly point on mainland Scotland?

5) What is the most southerly county in Wales?

6) Which is further south – the Mull of Galloway or Durham?

7) What isolated rock is the most westerly point of the British Isles?

8) What is the most westerly county on mainland Britain?

9) What is the most westerly point on the English mainland?

10) Grassholm, an island off the Pembrokeshire coast, and the most westerly part of Wales, has the world's fourth largest colony of which type of bird?

'Geography is about maps.'

E.C. BENTLEY

1) Near what cape are the Clo Mor cliffs, at 921 ft (281 m), the highest cliffs on mainland Britain?

2) What Hebridean island is the largest British island off mainland Britain?

3) What is the biggest English island?

4) What is the largest natural lake in mainland Britain, by surface area?

5) What is the largest artificial body of water in Britain, by surface area?

6) What is the largest natural lake in Wales?

7) What is the deepest lake in the Lake District?

8) What is the largest natural lake in England?

9) What town stands at the geographical centre of Scotland and is furthest from the sea?

10) What mountain village is the coldest place in Britain?

'Like all great travellers, I have seen more than I remember, and remember more than I have seen.'

BENJAMIN DISRAELI

1) What is Britain's longest river, 220 miles (354 km) in length?

2) What is the longest river in Scotland, 120 miles (193 km) in length?

3) What is the longest river that runs wholly within England and is 215 miles (346 km) in length?

4) Which county town sits on the River Towy, at 68 miles (109 km) long the longest river that flows wholly within Wales?

5) Which river has the highest source of any major river in Britain, at 4,000 ft (1,220 m)?

6) What is Wales's biggest bay?

7) In which Scottish county would you find Eas Coul Aulin, the highest waterfall in Britain, with a drop of 660 ft (200 m)?

8) In which English county would you find Oxlow Cavern, at 653 ft (199 m) in depth, the deepest cave in England?

9) What is the deepest gorge in Britain?

10) What is the lowest point in Britain?

Well, I Never Knew This!

Bhutan is the only country other than Wales to have a dragon on its flag.

'A man travels the world in search of what he needs and returns home to find it.'

GEORGE MOORE

1) What is the largest historic county in Britain?

2) What is Scotland's largest historic county?

3) What is England's third largest county?

4) What is the biggest city in Wales?

5) Is Cambridge in the eastern or western hemisphere?

6) Name the six official cities of Scotland (not cathedral cities).

7) Apart from the City of London, what is the smallest city in England?

8) What is the highest village in England?

9) What is Britain's third largest metropolis in terms of population?

10) What is England's most easterly county town?

HISTORY

'We cannot escape history.'

ABRAHAM LINCOLN

'History will be kind to me, for I intend to write it.'

Sir Winston Churchill

1) 'No freeman shall be seized, or imprisoned, or disseised, or outlawed, or any way destroyed, nor will we go upon him, nor will we send upon him, except by the lawful judgement of his peers or the law of the land.' Where do these words come from?

2) Which came first, the Battle of Naseby or the Battle of Edgehill?

3) Which Scottish king marched his army to Dover in 1215, further south than any king of Scots before or since?

4) Which northern city was granted a charter by King Alfred in 886, making it Britain's oldest city?

5) Who was the last monarch to be born in Scotland?

6) The Dunkirk evacuation of 1940 was organised from secret tunnels beneath which castle?

7) Who published a pamphlet entitled 'The First Blast of the Trumpet against the Monstrous Regiment of Women'?

8) Who was the first English Prince of Wales NOT to become king?

9) Which band leader was last seen alive taking off from an isolated Bedfordshire airfield in December 1944?

10) Who was the last woman to be hanged in Britain?

Well, I Never Knew This!

Not a single British ship was lost at the Battle of Trafalgar.

'There is a history in all men's lives.'

WILLIAM SHAKESPEARE

1) The design of the Scottish royal standard, a red lion rampant on a yellow background, came from the standard of which Scottish king?

2) Where in Britain did the Roman emperors Severus and Constantius die?

3) Which king faced down the Peasants' Revolt in 1381?

4) What year was the Battle of Stamford Bridge?

5) Near which small coastal town did the last invasion of the British mainland take place, in 1797?

6) Which is the oldest commissioned ship in the Royal Navy?

7) Who was the first person to be crowned Queen of England in her own right (not as the wife of a king)?

8) John Flamsteed was the first to occupy what position?

9) English place names ending in 'by', 'thorpe', 'thwaite' and 'beck' are a legacy of settlers from where?

10) Which city is considered the ecclesiastical capital of Wales?

Well, I Never Knew This!

The Union Flag is more commonly referred to as the Union Jack because it was initially flown only at sea, where flags were attached to the 'jack' staff at the ship's bow.

'History is merely gossip.'

OSCAR WILDE

1) Who was found hiding in a ditch in Dorset after defeat at the Battle of Sedgemoor in 1685?

2) Which castle was Edward II on his way to relieve when he was defeated at the Battle of Bannockburn by Robert the Bruce in 1314?

3) Durovernum was the Roman name for which British city?

4) Who was Scotland's partner in the 'Auld Alliance'?

5) What legendary figure was said to be the dispossessed Earl of Huntingdon?

6) Which Welsh port did Lord Nelson describe as 'the finest port in Christendom'?

7) What age were both the Duke of Cumberland and Bonnie Prince Charlie at the Battle of Culloden in 1746?

8) Which was the only one of Henry VIII's wives to outlive him?

9) What English city boasted Britain's first local radio station, opened in 1967?

10) Where did the Scotii, Kings of Dalriada, originally come from?

Well, I Never Knew This!

Lord Darnley, father of James I who was the target of the Gunpowder Plot in 1605, was himself assassinated in a plot using gunpowder.

Which British monarch . . . ?

1) enjoyed the longest reign of any British monarch?

2) was the last to lead troops into battle?

3) was the last monarch to be King of Ireland?

4) is the longest living?

5) was the first of the House of Windsor?

6) was known as the 'Sailor King'?

7) abdicated?

8) was the shortest king in height?

9) was the first to live in Buckingham Palace?

10) died as a result of his horse stumbling over a molehill?

11) began Westminster Abbey?

12) was probably murdered, in the Tower of London?

13) set up the Order of the Garter?

14) is buried somewhere in Faversham, Kent?

15) founded Eton?

16) died of a surfeit of lampreys?

17) was known as 'Longshanks'?

18) was deposed by the Glorious Revolution of 1688?

19) was shot by Walter Tyrell?

20) was the last English king to die in battle?

Well, I Never Knew This!

The first monarch to order boots specifically designed for each foot, as opposed to being made to wear on either foot, was George IV.

Which Scottish monarch . . . ?

1) was known as Canmore, or 'Big Head'?

2) married Mary of Guise?

3) was the last to be buried on Iona?

4) is considered the first King of Scots?

5) was the son of Robert the Bruce?

6) was murdered in Perth?

7) was chosen by Edward I of England?

8) married a Dauphin?

9) was killed by his own exploding cannon?

10) fell over a cliff and died when his horse stumbled?

Well, I Never Knew This!

It took 15 strokes of the axe to sever the head of Mary, Queen of Scots.

Which prime minister . . .

1) did Harold Wilson describe as 'an elegant anachronism'?

2) was the first Scotsman to serve as prime minister?

3) went to the same school in Scotland as James Bond?

4) was nearly blinded by a ginger biscuit thrown at him while he was riding in his open carriage?

5) died at Brocket Hall, allegedly on the billiard table in the arms of a chambermaid?

6) is the longest serving prime minister?

7) opened the Preston bypass on the M6, the first stretch of motorway, in 1958?

8) allegedly liked HP sauce all over his food?

9) gave his name to the capital of the state of Victoria?

10) was the richest ever prime minister?

Well, I Never Knew This!

The 3rd Duke of Grafton, prime minister from 1768–70, was a direct descendant of Charles II by the Merrie Monarch's mistress Barbara, Duchess of Cleveland.

Which prime minister was known as . . .

1) The Iron Lady?

2) The Iron Duke?

3) Bambi?

4) The Dormouse at the Tea Party?

5) 'Orange' and 'Lemon'?

6) Supermac?

7) The Grand Old Man?

8) The Big Clunking Fist?

9) Sunny Jim?

10) Attila the Hen?

Well, I Never Knew This!

Disraeli was a keen author. 'When I want to read a novel,' he said, 'I write one.'

Which prime minister was . . .

1) the only one to be assassinated in office?

2) the only one to wear a pince-nez?

3) the only Welsh prime minister?

4) the only one to have a type of footwear named after him?

5) the only one to die in No. 10?

6) the only one to serve four terms?

7) the only one born in a ladies' loo?

8) the only one born illegitimate?

9) the only serving prime minister to be interviewed by the police in a criminal investigation?

10) the only one born outside the British Isles?

Well, I Never Knew This!

After his death in 1965 Winston Churchill became the first person to appear on a British coin other than a monarch.

Margot Asquith, wife of Prime Minister Herbert Henry Asquith, and Sir Winston Churchill were both known for their waspish descriptions of others. Who were they talking about below?

Margot Asquith

1) '. . . if not a great man he was, at least, a great poster.'

2) '. . . very clever but sometimes his brains go to his head.'

3) 'He could not see a belt without hitting below it.'

4) 'He has a brilliant mind until he makes it up.'

And who said of Margot Asquith:

5) 'The affair between Margot Asquith and Margot Asquith will live as one of the prettiest love stories in all literature'?

Winston Churchill

6) 'A modest man who has much to be modest about.'

7) 'There, but for the grace of God, goes God.'

8) 'In defeat unbeatable, in victory unbearable.'

9) 'He occasionally stumbled over the truth, but hastily picked himself up and hurried on as though nothing had happened.'

And who said of Winston Churchill:

10) 'He is a man suffering from petrified adolescence.'

Below are some phrases that politicians never quite said or wish they hadn't. Who said, or is supposed to have said, the following?

1) 'I'm a pretty straight sort of guy . . .'

2) 'Peace in our time . . .'

3) 'Crisis? What crisis?'

4) 'There will be no loss of essential sovereignty.'

5) 'On yer bike.'

6) 'Every prime minister needs a Willie.'

7) 'We not only saved the world . . .'

8) 'This is not a time for soundbites . . . I feel the hand of history upon our shoulders . . .'

9) '. . . most of our people have never had it so good.'

10) 'Bastards!'

SPORT AND CULTURE

'The marriage of sport and
culture is Olympism.'

JUAN ANTONIO SAMARANCH

'Sports lubricate the body and the mind.'

BENJAMIN FRANKLIN

1) What national sporting venue lies at the foot of Cleeve Hill?

2) What was the name of the last English tennis player to win the Wimbledon men's singles title? BONUS QUESTION: How many singles titles did he win and in what years?

3) Name the five English Classic horse races.

4) Who was the golfer who sank the winning putt in the 1985 Ryder Cup that wrested the trophy away from the Americans for the first time in 28 years?

5) Which marquess, whose title comes from a mountain, sponsored the original 12 rules of boxing?

6) What football club was founded by Brother Walfrid?

7) What Neath-born soprano is the official mascot of the Welsh rugby team?

8) Who is the most successful jockey in the history of the Derby?

Well, I Never Knew This!

Golfer Jack Nicklaus is the only living person to have appeared on a Scottish banknote other than the Queen and the late Queen Mother. In 2005 the Royal Bank of Scotland issued a commemorative £5 note bearing his image in honour of Nicklaus's contribution to golf – he has won more majors than any other player in history (18).

9) Where was the world's first purpose-built motor-racing circuit?

10) Who was the youngest football player to appear for the England international team in the 20th century? BONUS QUESTION: And the oldest?

11) Which football team is nicknamed the 'Tractor Boys'?

12) At which racecourse is the Scottish Grand National run?

13) Who was the only person to hold the world land speed and world water speed records at the same time?

14) Which is the only non-English football team to win the FA Cup?

15) The rules of which sport were roughed out on the lawns of Nantclwyd House in Denbighshire by Major Walter Wingfield?

16) Who beat the All Blacks at Stradey Park in 1972?

17) Where did Stirling Moss win his first Grand Prix?

18) Who is the only European to have won the US Open Golf Championship since the end of World War Two?

Well, I Never Knew This!

The game of Snooker was named from the word used for new cadets at the Royal Military Academy at Woolwich. The game was devised in 1875 by army officer Sir Neville Chamberlain while he was serving in India. He referred to a hapless opponent who failed to pot a single ball while playing the new game as a 'snooker', and the name stuck.

19) What film immortalised the feat of Harold Abrahams, winner of the 100 metres gold medal at the 1924 Olympics in Paris?

20) Which former England international football striker, now a TV presenter, was never sent off during his professional playing career in England?

21) Which was the first British football team to win the European Cup?

22) Who was the first Sikh to represent England at cricket?

23) Who was the first Scot ever to play on the Centre Court at Wimbledon?

24) What was the first horse race to be filmed?

25) Who was the first footballer to be transferred for one million pounds?

26) Who was the first Briton to win the Indianapolis 500?

27) Which county did W. G. Grace play for?

28) Who are the only father and son both to have won the Formula One world motor racing championship?

29) What was the name of the first horse to win the Grand National?

30) In which city was the first international rugby match played in 1871 ?

31) Who was the first golfer to be knighted?

Well, I Never Knew This!

The first person to win world championships on both two wheels and four wheels was Englishman John Surtees in 1964.

32) Which yachtswoman, born in Reading in 1962, skippered the first all-female crew to enter the Whitbread Round the World Yacht Race, in 1990?

33) Which was the first English football club to go on foreign tour?

34) Who was the first English motor racing world champion?

35) Who was the first woman to train a Grand National winner? BONUS QUESTIONS: Which horse? In what year?

36) Who was the first person to swim the English Channel, in 1875?

37) Where was the first Open Championship played? BONUS QUESTION: In what year?

38) Who was the first person to run the mile in under four minutes?

39) Who was the first manager of the Scotland football team?

40) Who was the first person to drive at over 300 mph?

Well, I Never Knew This!

The first person to win gold medals at five consecutive Olympic Games was rower Steve Redgrave, who achieved the record at the 2000 games in Sydney, Australia.

'It was my Uncle George who discovered that alcohol was a food well in advance of modern medical thought.'

P.G. WODEHOUSE

1) What fruit was first grown in England at Dorney Court, in Buckinghamshire, for James I?

2) The secret recipe for which sauce was brought back from Bengal by a former governor, Lord Sandys?

3) What yellow-fleshed turnip was introduced into Scotland by entrepreneur Patrick Miller, who had been sent it by King Gustav of Sweden?

4) What is a Pontefract cake made of?

5) What uplifting kind of ingredient did Alexander McDougall from Dumfriesshire create?

6) Where was the first lager brewery in Britain?

7) What name connects a wartime leader and a dimpled whisky bottle?

8) For what invention that brings sparkle to our lives was Christopher Merrett, born in Gloucestershire in 1614, responsible – 30 years before a French monk, in fact?

9) What family from the Scottish Borders, who brought us the twin-set and pearls, indirectly gave their name to a snack that 'once you pop you can't stop'?

10) Where was Marmite first produced?

Well, I Never Knew This!

The world's most expensive bottle of wine was bought by the son of a Scotsman, millionaire publisher Malcolm Forbes, in 1985. He paid $160,000 (about £100,000) for a 1787 Château Lafite from the collection of the US President Thomas Jefferson, whose initials were engraved on the bottle. Apparently the cork later fell in, making the wine undrinkable.

'There is music in the air, music all around us . . .'

EDWARD ELGAR

1) 'Blessed is a world that sings. Gentle are its songs.' These words are the motto for what annual international celebration of music and verse?

2) Who was inspired to write an overture by a visit to Staffa?

3) 'Summer Is Icumin In', the first known English song, was written by a monk at which abbey, in 1240?

4) Which singer, born in Llandaff, is the youngest artist ever to top the classical charts?

5) For what did Ben Jonson write the words and John Bull write the music – allegedly?

6) *Tubular Bells*, composed by Mike Oldfield, born in Reading in 1953, was the first album released by which record label?

7) David Byrne, who was born in Dumbarton in 1952, and appeared as himself in an episode of *The Simpsons* in 2003, was a lead member of which band?

8) Which Spice Girl was born in Goff's Oak, Hertfordshire, in 1974?

9) Which Scottish entertainer included amongst his best-loved songs, 'Roamin' in the Gloamin'' and 'Keep Right On To The End Of The Road'?

10) Who has written more music for James Bond films than any other composer?

Well, I Never Knew This!

Gustav Holst refused to compose a movement for the planet Pluto, which was only discovered in 1930, long after he had finished writing his suite *The Planets*. Pluto has since been redefined as a 'dwarf' planet.

'Lay aside life-harming heaviness and entertain a cheerful disposition.'

WILLIAM SHAKESPEARE

1) What was filmed at Carnforth railway station in 1945?

2) Which Hollywood actor bought himself a wedding ring of Welsh gold to celebrate his marriage to a Welsh girl in 2000?

3) Which politician married actress Valerie Hobson as his second wife?

4) What did British-born actor James Stewart call himself in order to avoid being confused with the American-born actor James 'Jimmy' Stewart?

5) Who decapitated a statue with his bowler hat after his master had lost a golf match to James Bond filmed at Stoke Poges Golf Club (below)?

6) What port, once home to the biggest steelworks in Europe, inspired Ridley Scott's vision for the future in his 1982 film *Blade Runner*?

7) What actress gave the longest ever Oscar acceptance speech, 7 minutes long?

8) What did Richard Burton and Elizabeth Taylor film in Fishguard in 1972?

9) In what film did the windmill above Turville in Buckinghamshire play the home of Caractacus Potts?

10) What detective was portrayed on television in the 1960s by Rupert Davies (below), buried at Pistyl on the Lleyn Peninsula?

'I believe entertainment can aspire to be art,
and can become art, but if you set out to make art,
you're an idiot.'

STEVE MARTIN

1) From where in Wales did Tom Cruise's great-great-grandfather emigrate to America?

2) Where would you find the Cobb, where Meryl Streep posed in profile for the film version of *The French Lieutenant's Woman*?

3) Where was David Frost born?

4) In which film, based on a novel by Edith Nesbit, was Three Chimneys, home of the lead characters, portrayed by Bents Farm near Bradford?

5) For which film did Dame Judi Dench (below) win an Oscar for portraying Elizabeth I on screen for just eight minutes?

6) The television adaptation of Anthony Trollope's *Barchester Chronicles* was filmed around which cathedral? BONUS QUESTION: Which queen is buried there?

7) For which two films did Glenda Jackson win her Oscars?

8) What kind of comedies are *Kind Hearts and Coronets*, *Passport to Pimlico* and *The Lavender Hill Mob*?

9) What cult television series was filmed at Portmeirion? BONUS QUESTIONS: Who played the lead role and in what series did he star previously?

10) Where would you find the largest sound stage in the world?

How are the following actors and entertainers better known?

1) Krishna Bhanji

2) Emma Bunton

3) Maurice Joseph Micklewhite

4) Arthur Stanley Jefferson

5) Gordon Sumner

6) David McDonald

7) Michael Dumbbell-Smith

8) Richard Walter Jenkins

9) William Pratt

10) David Ivor Davis

Well, I Never Knew This!

Alfred Hitchcock gave the shortest-ever Oscar acceptance speech when he accepted the Irving Thalberg Memorial Award in 1967. He simply said, 'Thank You.'

'A book's a book, though there's nothing in't.'

LORD BYRON

1) What brotherhood did Holman Hunt belong to?

2) The first English artist to be made a peer and the first English actor to win an Oscar were both born in the first English seaside resort – where is it? BONUS QUESTION: What were their names?

3) Where was Mary Shelley living when she wrote *Frankenstein*?

4) Which English novelist joined the Monmouth Rebellion of 1685?

5) The lakeland portrait painter George Romney gives his name to a brand of what product, taken to the top of Mount Everest by Hilary and Tensing?

6) Who wrote *Chitty Chitty Bang Bang*?

7) Which big friendly author was baptised at the Norwegian church in Cardiff in 1916?

8) Which author and Oxford professor died on the same day that JFK was assassinated?

9) The last work of Sir Edward Burne-Jones was a stained-glass window honouring which prime minister who had died only a few weeks before he did?

10) Which Scottish author spent his last years on Samoa?

Well, I Never Knew This!

The longest overdue book known about in the world was a biography of the Archbishop of Bremen borrowed from the library of Sidney Sussex College, Cambridge, in 1668, and discovered 288 years later, in 1956, at Houghton Hall in Norfolk – the home of Britain's first prime minister, Sir Robert Walpole.

'What has reason to do with . . . art . . .?'

WILLIAM BLAKE

1) What literary home is thought to have been inspired by Mapledurham House beside the River Thames?

2) England's first police force, the Bow Street Runners, was the brainchild of which writer, whose work made Jonathan Swift laugh for one of only two times in his life?

3) Who is the most quoted female author in the *Oxford English Dictionary*?

4) Which author had his ashes scattered at the old school he hated, the King's School, Canterbury?

5) Who was England's first professional female novelist and spy, and author of *Oroonoko*?

BONUS QUESTION: Where is she buried?

6) Who created Dr Doolittle?

7) Which novel was the subject of a celebrated trial that rewrote the obscenity laws in 1960? BONUS QUESTION: Who wrote it?

8) Who wrote the first Gothic novel at his Gothic house of Strawberry Hill? BONUS QUESTION: What is the novel called?

9) Which author had a son with H.G. Wells?

10) Richard Wilson, regarded by many as the 'Father of British landscape painting', is buried beside the church in which Welsh county town?

Well, I Never Knew This!

The word bible does not appear in any of Shakespeare's works.

'Reading is to the mind what exercise is to the body.'

SIR RICHARD STEELE

1) What famous school did Ronald Searle base on a girls' school in Edinburgh?

2) The Hogsmill was the setting for which painting by Millais?

3) In which novel does 'She who must be obeyed' appear? BONUS QUESTION: Who wrote it?

4) What is the great work of historian Edward Gibbon, who was buried in Fletching in 1794?

5) Which novels did John Bunyan, Thomas Malory and John Cleland each write while they were in prison?

6) Who painted *The Blue Boy*?

7) Who was the first English-born artist to be knighted? BONUS QUESTION: And which artist became his son-in-law?

8) What was compiled by the Revd Dr Ebenezer Cobham Brewer, buried in the churchyard of Edwinstowe Church, where the fabled Robin Hood is said to have married Maid Marian?

9) Who wrote *Three Men in a Boat*?

10) Which novel begins 'Last night I dreamt I went to Manderley again'?

Well, I Never Knew This!

Jane Austen dedicated *Emma* to her admirer the Prince Regent even though she thoroughly disapproved of his lifestyle.

What is the pen name of each of the following authors?

1) Eric Arthur Blair

2) David Cornwell

3) Joseph Korzeniowski

4) Mary Siepman

5) Charles Dodgson

6) Cecil Smith

7) John Burgess Wilson

8) Hector Hugh Munro

9) Arthur Quiller-Couch

10) James Alfred Wight

Well, I Never Knew This!

The surname Cockburn, as in Cockburn's port, is the only example in the English language of a word that uses a silent 'ck'.

What do the following authors' initials stand for?

1) C.S. Lewis

2) J.R.R. Tolkien

3) J.K. Rowling

4) P.G. Wodehouse

5) A.N. Wilson

6) P. D. James

7) E.F. Benson

8) T.E. Lawrence

9) D.H. Lawrence

10) H.G. Wells

'Poetry is the spontaneous overflow of powerful feelings . . . recollected in tranquility.'

WILLIAM WORDSWORTH

1) Benjamin Britten based his *War Requiem* on the poems of which poet who died in the First World War?

2) Where did Dylan Thomas get 'off the bus and forget to get on again'?

3) Who was known as the Ettrick Shepherd?

4) What village was Rupert Brooke dreaming of when he wrote: 'Stands the church clock at ten to three? And is there honey still for tea?' BONUS QUESTION: Who lives in the Old Vicarage there now?

5) Lord Byron was the cousin of which prime minister?

6) What kind of tree did Alexander Pope introduce into England?

7) What kind of creature did Robert Burns describe as a 'wee, sleekit, cowrin', tim'rous beastie'?

8) What was the name of Sebastian Flyte's teddy bear in *Brideshead Revisited*, which was inspired by Sir John Betjeman's teddy bear Archibald?

9) What hills did Wordsworth and Coleridge stride across while discussing *The Lyrical Ballads*?

10) What waterfall was George Borrow referring to when he wrote 'I never saw water falling so gracefully . . .'?

Complete the following lines of poetry.
For a bonus – who wrote them?

1) If I should die think only this of me,
   That there's some corner of a foreign field . . .
   (5 words)

2) They shall grow not old . . .
   (7 words)

3) What is this life if, full of care . . .
   (8 words)

4) In Xanadu did Kubla Khan . . .
   (5 words)

5) None but the brave . . .
   (3 words)

6) The curfew tolls the knell of parting day
   The lowing herd wind slowly o'er the lea
   The ploughman . . .
   (5 words)

7) I wandered lonely as a cloud
   That floats on high o'er vales and hills
   When all at once I saw a crowd . . .
   (5 words)

8) Under the bludgeonings of chance
   My head is . . .
   (3 words)

9) There's a breathless hush . . .
   (4 words)

10) How do I love thee? . . .
    (5 words)

Well, I Never Knew This!

Lord Byron was a member of the Harrow team that took part in the first Eton v. Harrow cricket match at Lord's in 1805.

FIRSTS AND SECONDS

'. . . nothing should ever be done
for the first time.'

F.M. CORNFORD

There's always a first time . . .

1) In which town would you find Murdock House, the first in the world to be lit by gas?

2) Who was the first woman to be admitted to the Order of Merit?

3) Who was the world's first tour operator? BONUS QUESTION: Where did the first ever package tour go to?

4) Where did Locomotion Number One finish its historic journey on 27 September 1825?

5) Which chocolate maker made the world's first solid chocolate and the world's first edible chocolate bar?

6) What was Britain's first National Park, opened in 1951?

7) Who gave her name to a pudding and, in 1920, was the first professional artiste to broadcast on the radio in Britain?

8) With what world first did Joseph Swan illuminate his home in Gateshead in 1878?

9) Who built the world's first factory complex at Cromford in Derbyshire in 1771?

Well, I Never Knew This!

The first British monarch to visit America was George VI in 1939.

10) Who was the first Archbishop of Canterbury?

11) MP William Huskisson was the first high-profile victim in the world of what type of accident?

12) Which Scottish university took in Britain's first female student?

13) Which king had to agree to the Provisions of Oxford, the first official document of its kind to be written in English? BONUS QUESTION: What two other languages was it written in as well as English?

14) Who was the first person to use the 'f' word on British television?

15) Who was the first brewer to settle in Burton-on-Trent, in 1777?

16) Who was the first man to be officially called Prime Minister?

17) Where would you find Britain's first statue to a woman who was not royal? BONUS QUESTION: Who is it a statue of?

18) William Dampier, born and buried in East Coker in Somerset, was the first Englishman to set foot where?

19) Which National Trust house in Hampshire was the first in England to have a classical portico?

Well, I Never Knew This!

The first computer to appear on a stamp was Charles Babbage's Analytical Engine, which was never actually built because of the limitations of the mechanical tools of the day.

20) What is the name of the world's first test-tube baby, who was born in Oldham in 1978?

21) What is the earliest public record of England that exists?

22) Where was Britain's first official nudist beach?

23) What was the world's first adhesive postage stamp called?

24) Who invented the world's first production line at his Soho works in Handsworth, Birmingham?

25) What make of car was the first to go over 100 mph (160 kph)? BONUS QUESTION: Where is the ancestral home of the man who built the car?

26) What was Ian Fleming's first James Bond novel?

27) Which was the first stately home in England to be opened to the public?

28) Cadmeon, who wrote the first English poetry, was a cowherd at which abbey?

29) Who built the world's first colour television?

Well, I Never Knew This!

The first frozen meat was actually Bacon – the philosopher and statesman, Sir Francis Bacon (1561–1626). In 1626, in Highgate, he stuffed a chicken with snow to see if it would help preserve the meat – but unfortunately got pneumonia and died a few days later.

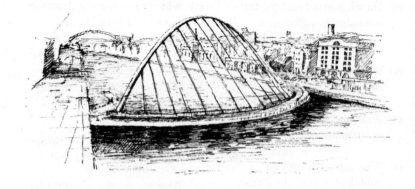

30) A member of which Scottish family, associated with a gin, a setter, a gay dance and a prime minister, was America's first known millionaire?

31) Where was designated as Britain's first Area of Outstanding Natural Beauty in 1956?

32) Where was the first ever Labour Prime Minister, Ramsay MacDonald born in 1866?

33) In 1953 Lita Roza became the first woman to reach No. 1 in the charts, with what song?

34) In which city can you find the world's first public park, the Arboretum, opened in 1840, and the world's first silk mill, opened in 1721?

35) Which was the first city in Britain to introduce a congestion charge, in 2002?

36) Who was the first man to fly across the English Channel in both directions? BONUS QUESTION: Who was the first Briton to be killed in an air accident?

37) What river is spanned by the world's first tilting bridge?

38) On what island was the first compulsory education in Britain introduced in 1834?

39) What building was the first in Britain to have latrines?

40) Who was the first Englishman to circumnavigate the world?

41) Who compiled the first published atlas of the British Isles?

42) Where in London were the first speed bumps introduced in 1984?

43) Which was the first Cambridge college?

44) In 1810, in a small cottage in Ruthwell, Dumfriesshire, the Revd Henry Duncan opened the first what?

45) Which town was the departure point for the world's first railway journey by the world's first steam locomotive in 1804?

46) John Davis was the first European to see what group of islands, in 1592?

47) At which university was Britain's first student union formed?

48) What was the first planned village in England, begun in 1771?

49) What stretch of water is crossed by the Britannia Bridge, the world's first major tubular bridge?

50) Which was the first Cistercian abbey in Scotland?

Well, I Never Knew This!

Britain's first parking ticket was handed out in 1960, slapped on to the windscreen of a Ford Popular belonging to Dr Thomas Creighton, who had parked outside a London hotel to help a man suffering from a heart attack. After a public outcry he was eventually let off.

51) Where in 1566 was Britain's first recorded public fireworks display put on to celebrate the christening of the future James VI of Scotland?

52) Where in 1586 did Sir John Spilman set up England's first commercial paper mill?

53) The first European meeting of which organisation was held in Llanfair PG in 1915?

54) The first bombs dropped on Britain in the Second World War fell on what part of Scotland?

55) Which Jedburgh daughter of the manse became the first 'scientist' when William Whewell invented the term in a review of her tract 'On the Connexion of the Sciences', in 1834? An Oxford college is named after her.

56) Beatrix Potter's father was the first life member of what organisation?

57) What dance was first introduced into England at Brocket Hall in Hertfordshire? BONUS QUESTION: By whom?

58) Where was Scotland's first dry dock – the same tongue-twisting place where the police dismisseth us?

59) Who was the first man to fly under Tower Bridge – he was also the holder of Pilot's Licence No. 1.

Well, I Never Knew This!

The first criminal to be convicted using DNA evidence was Robert Melias who was found guilty of rape at Bristol Crown Court in November 1987. Britain now has by far the largest DNA database in the world with over 5 million people on it (as of 2009).

60) Kitty, the Red Duchess, was the first Scottish woman MP and first female Conservative cabinet member – of where was she the Duchess?

61) What is the ancestral home of the first Scotsman to become Lord Chancellor, Lord Mansfield?

62) Skokholm Island off the coast of Pembrokeshire is home to Britain's first what, established by naturalist Ronald Lockley in 1933?

63) Who was the first Englishman, and the youngest person, ever to win a Nobel Prize for Literature?

64) Who was the first person to write extensively in English and the first historian to date events from the Year of Our Lord, Anno Domini (AD)?

65) What railway was the first narrow-gauge railway in the world to carry passengers, in 1863?

66) Who was England's first black archbishop?

67) What was Scotland's first Conservation Village?

68) For what political party was Gwynfor Evans the first elected MP, for Carmarthen in 1966?

69) What name is shared by Scotland's first protestant martyr and the first man to fly over Mount Everest?

70) What was the first capital of England?

Well, I Never Knew This!

Two different Scotsmen claim to have invented the cash dispenser and PIN number system – John Shepherd-Barron from Tain in Ross & Cromarty and James Goodfellow from Paisley, Renfrewshire.

71) Who was the first Stuart monarch? BONUS QUESTION: And the last?

72) Where was the first National Eisteddfod held in 1176?

73) Tomatoes were first grown in England in the country's first conservatory at which stately home?

74) Robert Bontine Cunninghame Graham, first president of the Scottish Labour party, was also the first man to be suspended from the House of Commons for swearing. What was the offending word he used?

75) The world's first million-pound deal was struck at the Coal Exchange in which Welsh city?

76) Where in Britain is the site of the world's first fast-breeder nuclear reactor?

77) Where in Britain was the world's first dry dock built in 1495?

78) What was the first capital of Roman Britain?

79) What was made UNESCO's first City of Literature, in 2004?

80) Where in Wales is Britain's first comprehensive school?

Well, I Never Knew This!

While the Penny Black was the first postage stamp, the first postage stamp with a perforated edge was the Penny Red, issued in 1854.

81) In which county was the first holiday camp in England opened?

82) Who performed the very first Christian coronation in Britain, at Dunadd in 574?

83) Who was the first Welsh leader of the Labour Party?

84) What was the first neo-gothic castle to be built in Britain?

85) What weapon, designed and developed in Lincoln, was first used in combat at the Battle of the Somme in 1916?

86) James Isbister became the first person to be killed on British soil in the Second World War during a bombing raid on what part of Scotland?

87) Who printed Anthony Woodville's translation from the French of *The Sayings of the Philosophers* in 1476, the first book ever printed in England?

88) The Roxburghe Club, formed in 1812, was the first club of its kind in the world – what sort of club is it?

89) Scots-American Ebenezer Munro fired the first shot of which war?

90) Who was the first Protestant Archbishop of Canterbury? BONUS QUESTION: Who was the last Roman Catholic Archbishop of Canterbury?

Well, I Never Knew This!

Britain's first number plate, A1, was secured in 1903 by Earl Russell for his Napier, after he had queued all night outside the London County Council offices.

On second thoughts . . .

1) Where is known as the second-hand bookshop capital of the world?

2) What cathedral boasts the second highest spire in England?

3) What is the second largest ruined cathedral in Scotland?

4) What is Scotland's second oldest university?

5) Which castle vies with Arundel as the second largest inhabited castle in England?

6) What house in Norfolk was built by Britain's first prime minister as his second home?

7) What is Britain's second largest city, by population?

8) Who was the second golfer to be knighted?

9) What is England's second oldest bishopric, created in 604?

10) What is Britain's second oldest university?

And ultimately . . .

1) In which city would you find the Midland Hotel, oldest railway hotel in the world, opened in 1840?

2) In the courtyard of which palace might you see the oldest fountain in Britain, recently restored?

3) Which English abbey has the largest Norman tower in the world?

4) What are the oldest regalia in Europe known as?

5) In the grounds of which castle would you find the Pharos, the tallest item of Roman remains in Britain?

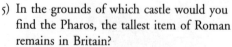

6) What is the smallest breed of English terrier?

7) Scotland's oldest distillery, the Glenturret distillery in Perthshire, produces which whisky, the best-selling whisky in Britain?

8) In which county town would you find High House, the largest remaining timber-framed town house in England?

9) Down on the quay of which Welsh town can you find the smallest house in Britain, just 10 ft 2 inches (3.1 m) high and 5 ft (1.8 m) wide?

10) The clock tower of which ducal pile is home to the oldest carillon of bells in England? BONUS QUESTION: The home of which Duke?

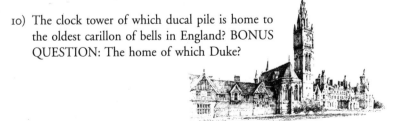

BUILDINGS OF BRITAIN

'We shape our buildings;
thereafter they shape us.'

SIR WINSTON CHURCHILL

Name the cathedral

1) Which English cathedral was the first building in the world to be constructed higher than the Great Pyramid?

2) Where is the most northerly cathedral in Britain?

3) Which is the longest medieval cathedral in the world?

4) Where would you go to find Britain's smallest medieval cathedral?

5) Which minster, which dominates the cathedral town that gave us the Bramley apple, is proud of its stone 'leaves'?

6) Which is England's smallest cathedral?

7) To which saint is Glasgow's medieval cathedral dedicated?

8) Which Welsh cathedral occupies the oldest cathedral site still in use in Britain?

9) Near which cathedral was Britain's youngest ever Davis Cup player born?

10) Which cathedral is a shrine to England's first Christian martyr?

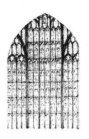

11) Which cathedral contains the largest stained glass window in Britain, the Crecy Window?

12) In which cathedral did pop star Madonna have her son Rocco christened in December 2000?

13) In which medieval Welsh cathedral would you find Britain's biggest cresset stone?

14) Which cathedral boasts a medieval painted ceiling that is unique in Britain and the longest of its kind in Europe?

15) Where in Scotland would you go to find the only granite medieval cathedral in the world?

'England's churches are the highest expressions of the art and architecture of their age.'

1) In what county would you find All Saints, Brixworth, the largest surviving Saxon church in England?

2) The benefactor of which university lies in a tomb outside the west door of St Giles Church in Wrexham?

3) What town is known for Mint Cake and the widest parish church in England?

4) In what county would you find All Saints, Earls Barton, which has the finest Saxon tower in Britain?

5) The football club of which Scottish town takes its name from the church where John Knox gave a famous sermon which precipitated the Reformation in Scotland in 1558?

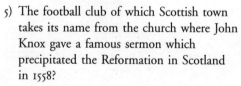

6) What church did Elizabeth I describe as 'the fairest, goodliest and most famous parish church in England'?

7) Which hilly county town in North Wales is the home of Capel Pendref, the first purpose-built Wesleyan chapel in Wales?

8) The brass of Sir John D'Abernon in Stoke D'Abernon Church is not only the oldest brass in England but also the only one to show a knight with a what?

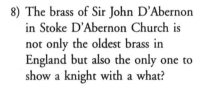

9) In which county would you find St Andrew's church, Greensted, which dates possibly from the 9th century and is the oldest wooden church in the world?

10) Normanton Church in Rutland was half drowned by the rising waters of England's largest man-made lake, which is called what?

Name the castle

1) Which Suffolk castle was the first in England to be built without a keep?

2) A statue of which controversial ghillie can be found, with difficulty, hidden in a remote part of the grounds at Balmoral?

3) Which English castle boasts the largest keep ever built in Europe?

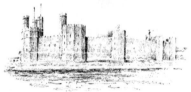

4) The walls of Caernarfon Castle were designed to resemble the walls of which great city?

5) Henry VII's eldest son Arthur lived at Ludlow Castle with his wife – who was she?

6) Which castle in Aberdeenshire
is the oldest intact building in
the care of the National Trust
for Scotland?

7) What is the largest castle in Wales?

8) Which castle, built by Henry II in
1180, was the first concentric castle in
England?

9) Which castle sits on a rock
described by the Venerable Bede
as 'the best fortified city the
Britons had'?

10) Which Welsh castle is
approached by smaller
prototypes of the two great
bridges across the Menai Strait?

11) The grounds of which ruined castle are now home to Scotland's largest leisure park?

12) Who was murdered with a red-hot poker in Berkeley Castle in Gloucestershire – allegedly?

13) Who was Castle Coch built for?

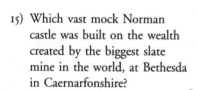

14) In which Scottish castle, renowned for its Jacobean painted ceilings, would you find the 'Horn of Leys', given to the Burnett family's ancestors by Robert the Bruce?

15) Which vast mock Norman castle was built on the wealth created by the biggest slate mine in the world, at Bethesda in Caernarfonshire?

Name the bridge

1) Where would you find the 'bridge by the earthen house' which, for a long time, was the longest single stone arch in the world?

2) You might cross Tickford Bridge in Newport Pagnell, the oldest iron bridge in Britain still carrying heavy traffic, in order to visit the factory where what make of car is made?

3) Ralph Wood threw himself to his death off the bridge he had just built – the first railway bridge in the world and for 50 years the longest single span in Britain – because he thought it would fall down. What is the name of that bridge?

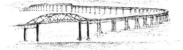

4) Which river is crossed by the longest railway bridge in Britain?

5) In which county would you find Poohsticks Bridge?

Well, I Never Knew This!

The central span of Britain's longest suspension bridge, the Humber Bridge, is so long that the tops of the two bridge towers are nearly one and a half inches (36 mm) further apart at the top than at the bottom, to take account of the curvature of the earth.

6) Iron Bridge, the first bridge in the world to be made from iron, was built in what year?

7) The Barmouth Railway Bridge, built in 1867, crosses which estuary?

8) Which Cambridge college can boast of a 'Bridge of Sighs'?

9) Who built the 'Sounding Arch' at Maidenhead, the widest, flattest brick arch in the world?

10) In what film can Tom Cruise be seen clinging to the top of a train while it is speeding across Ballochmyle Viaduct in Ayrshire, the highest railway bridge in Britain?

Well, I Never Knew This!

The earliest surviving concrete bridge in the world crosses the River Axe at Seaton in Devon and was built as a toll bridge in 1877.

THERE'S NO PLACE LIKE HOME

—᪥᪥᪥᪥᪥(◉)᪥᪥᪥᪥᪥—

'Home is where the heart is.'

ANON

Who was born here?

1) Hayes Barton, Devon in
1552 – he found a new world
but lost a colony.

2) Cockermouth in 1770 – did he
come trailing clouds of glory?

3) An auld clay biggin in Alloway
in 1759 – should auld
acquaintance be forgot?

4) Elstow, Bedfordshire in 1628 – he awoke,
and behold it was a dream.

5) Wylam, Northumberland in
1781 – he gave us a Rocket.

6) Grantham in 1925 – we are a grandmother.

7) Lichfield in 1709 – a man of many words.

8) Ickwell Green, Bedfordshire in 1639 – England's Father Time.

9) Higher Bockhampton, Dorset in 1840 – far from the madding crowd?

10) Ecclefechan in 1795 – the Sage of Chelsea.

Who lived here?

1) Buckland Abbey, Devon – two Elizabethan sailors, one famous for his Revenge and the other for his Drum?

2) The Wakes, Selborne, Hampshire – author of the first Natural History of England?

3) Major Oak, Nottinghamshire – a dispossessed Earl, perhaps?

4) Woolsthorpe Manor – quite a windfall?

5) Plas Newydd, Llangollen – not gentlemen?

6) Morton's Tower, Lambeth Palace –
gateway to the London home of this
Primate?

7) A cottage in Shottery,
Warwickshire – her husband
became the most quoted man
in the *Oxford English
Dictionary*?

8) Chawton, Hampshire – it took
some Persuasion for Emma
there . . . ?

9) Dove Cottage, Grasmere,
Westmorland – a golden host?

10) Wrotham Park,
Hertfordshire – he was
shot 'pour encourager
les autres'?

11) Haworth Parsonage – Ellis Bell and her sisters, maybe?

12) Newstead Abbey – mad, bad and dangerous to know!

13) Cloud's Hill – built on the Seven Pillars of Wisdom, perhaps?

14) Headington Hill Hall – a bit overboard for a council house?

15) Tredegar House, Newport, Monmouthshire – bit of a rum family? Or was it sports cars?

16) A cottage in Chalfont St Giles,
Buckinghamshire – paradise lost?

17) Greenway, Devon – a woman
of mystery?

18) Cliveden House,
Buckinghamshire –
would she really put
poison in her
husband's tea?

19) Crosby Hall, Chelsea – his own Utopia,
perhaps?

20) Kelmscott Manor – this one made
wallpaper, not cars?

MATCHBOX

'Here's a nice bit of boxed fruit.'
P.G. WODEHOUSE

Which cathedral?

Below are five descriptions and four cathedrals. Match the description to the cathedral and there will be one description left. What cathedral does that description refer to?

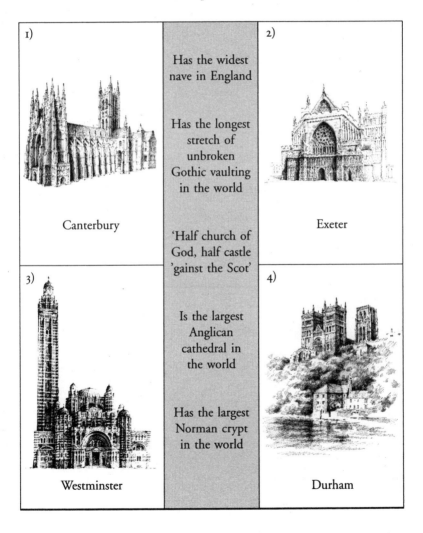

1) Canterbury

2) Exeter

Has the widest nave in England

Has the longest stretch of unbroken Gothic vaulting in the world

'Half church of God, half castle 'gainst the Scot'

Is the largest Anglican cathedral in the world

Has the largest Norman crypt in the world

3) Westminster

4) Durham

Below are five more descriptions and four more cathedrals. Again, match the description to the cathedral and there will be one description left. What cathedral does that description refer to?

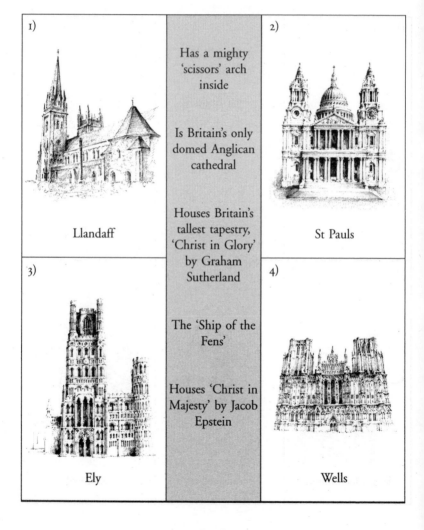

1) Llandaff

2) St Pauls

3) Ely

4) Wells

Has a mighty 'scissors' arch inside

Is Britain's only domed Anglican cathedral

Houses Britain's tallest tapestry, 'Christ in Glory' by Graham Sutherland

The 'Ship of the Fens'

Houses 'Christ in Majesty' by Jacob Epstein

Inventions

Below are five inventions and four inventors. Match the invention to the inventor and there will be one invention left. Who invented that?

1)	Jethro Tull	2)
	Edwin Budding	
	Thomas Newcomen	
	Daniel Albone	
Tractor		Lawn mower

3)	4)	5)
Steam locomotive	Steam engine	Seed drill

Below are five more inventions and four more inventors. Again, match the invention to the inventor and there will be one invention left. Who invented that?

1)		2)
Marine chronometer	William Symington Revd William Lee Sir Frank Whittle John Logie Baird	Television
3)	4)	5)
Steam boat	Jet	Stocking frame

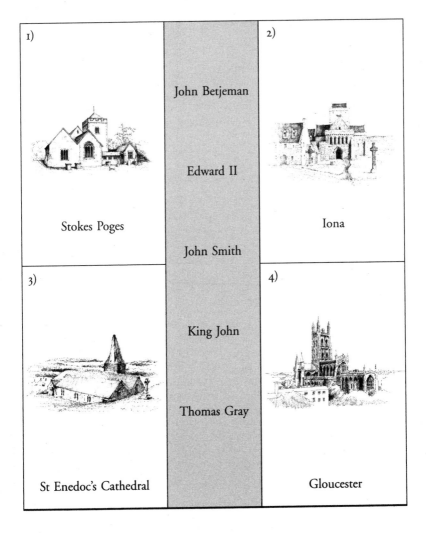

Who rests here?

Below are five characters from history and four burial sites. Match the character to their burial site and there will be one character left. Where is that character buried?

1)

Stokes Poges

John Betjeman

Edward II

John Smith

2)

Iona

3)

St Enedoc's Cathedral

King John

Thomas Gray

4)

Gloucester

COUNTIES OF BRITAIN

'The stories of the counties reveal their individuality – each has a personality and a corporate existence which is for the advantage of the nation . . . and enriches the national individuality.'

What do you know about Aberdeenshire?

1) Who is said to have based the design of his own fantasy castle on 'Danzig Willie' Forbes's Craigievar Castle (right)?

2) What flower was named after the Aberdeenshire-born botanist Alexander Garden?

3) Who laid the foundation of Crathie Church (below) in 1893?

4) What French killing machine was modelled on the 'Aberdeen Maiden' that killed the 4th Earl of Huntly in 1562 in front of a weeping Mary, Queen of Scots?

5) Which building in Aberdeen is the second largest granite building in the world after the Escorial in Madrid?

What do you know about Anglesey?

1) Who built the world's first
large-scale suspension bridge,
the Menai Bridge (right)?

2) Which is bigger – Anglesey or
the Isle of Wight?

3) The ancestors of which royal
house are buried in the village
church of St Gredifael on
Anglesey?

4) In which cult 1968 film does a
character called Dildano, played
by David Hemmings, use the
full name for Llanfair PG as a
password?

5) Which member of two comedy
partnerships was born in
Holyhead in 1957?

What do you know about Angus?

1) What was discovered beneath the altar of Arbroath Abbey (right) in 1951?

2) What is the name of the oldest British ship still afloat, launched at Chatham in 1824 and now moored at Dundee's City Quay?

3) Who was born at Glamis Castle (below) in 1930?

4) What was invented by James Chalmers, born in Arbroath in 1782?

5) James Graham, immortalised by Sir Walter Scott as 'Bonnie' Dundee, died leading James VII of Scotland's troops at which battle in 1689?

What do you know about Argyllshire?

1) What distinction is held by Corrachadh Mor on the Ardnamurchan Peninsula?

2) On what loch does Inverary Castle (right) sit?

3) The 'Wee Picture House' (below), opened in 1913 and now the oldest cinema in Scotland, can be found in the largest town on Kintyre – what town is that?

4) Where were at least 38 members of the MacDonald clan killed in the early hours of 13 February 1692?

5) Who was the captain of the *Vital Spark* in Hugh Foulis's novels? BONUS QUESTION: What was Hugh Foulis's real name?

What do you know about Ayrshire?

1) Which famous bridge can you see from the Burns Monument in Alloway (right)?

2) Which Ayrshire whisky brand has a 'striding man', drawn by artist Tom Browne, as its logo?

3) In which Ayrshire town would you find Scotland's oldest merchant's house, Loudoun Hall (below), built in 1513?

4) Ayrshire is the only county in Britain to boast three golf courses that have hosted the Open Championship. Name them.

5) Who was given tenure of an apartment at Culzean Castle in recognition of his wartime achievements?

What do you know about Banffshire?

1) Cullen House (right), once the seat of the Earls of Seafield, is not the only thing for which the little seaside town of Cullen is known – there is also Cullen Skink. What is Cullen Skink?

2) Which Banffshire whisky brand uses a unique triangular bottle, introduced in 1957?

3) Who built Craigellachie Bridge (below), Scotland's oldest iron bridge, across the Spey in 1814?

4) What house did the 1st Earl Fife commission from William Adam and then never set foot in because of a dispute over the cost?

5) What village, generally accepted as the highest village in the Highlands, was founded by the Duke of Gordon in 1750?

What do you know about Bedfordshire?

1) What is the name of the prison reformer and one-time High Sheriff of Bedfordshire who was the first commoner to be commemorated by a statue in St Paul's Cathedral?

2) Dunstable Priory (right), where the first play ever seen in England was performed, stands at the crossroads of the Icknield Way and what other ancient roadway?

3) Elstow Moot Hall (below) houses a museum dedicated to which writer?

4) The Cardington-born founder of which brewery, once the biggest in Britain, was the first man to speak out in Parliament against slavery?

5) The R101 airship, which on completion in October 1929 was the largest man-made object ever to fly, was built in Bedfordshire by which brothers?

What do you know about Berkshire?

1) Which king first built a castle at Windsor (right)?

2) Which play did William Shakespeare write for Elizabeth I while staying in Windsor?

3) Which Berkshire town is home to the world's largest lion (below)? BONUS QUESTION: Which king is buried in the town's abbey?

4) John Walter, who built Bear Wood House near Wokingham in 1865, was the founder of which newspaper?

5) Berkshire is the only English county that can boast of having what prefix to its name?

What do you know about Berwickshire?

1) What colour are the banisters of the main staircase at Manderston (right)?

2) Which son of Berwickshire founded the British Legion?

3) Which author is buried at Dryburgh Abbey (below)?

4) Which two towns tussled for 300 years to be county town of Berwickshire, and which finally succeeded in 1903?

5) Which river is spanned by Britain's first suspension bridge for vehicular traffic, the Union Chain Bridge?

What do you know about Breconshire?

1) Which opera singer, whose rendition of 'Home Sweet Home' reduced Abraham Lincoln to tears, lived at Craig-y-Nos (right)?

2) At which celebrated battle did the 24th Regiment of Foot, later renamed the South Wales Borderers, win seven Victoria Crosses, the largest number ever awarded to a single regiment for one action?

3) Which river is crossed at Crickhowell by the longest stone bridge in Wales (below)?

4) Which sculptor and artist set up a commune at Capel-y-Ffin and there designed the typeface Gill Sans, as used on the covers of pre-war Penguin books?

5) Which actress was born in Brecon in 1755?

What do you know about Buckinghamshire?

1) William Penn, who is buried outside Jordans Meeting House (right), founded which city, named from the Greek for 'brotherly love'?

2) Name the two inns on the A5 in Stony Stratford that give their names to an unlikely or exaggerated story?

3) What was cracked at Bletchley Park (below)?

4) What newsagent do you associate with the village of Hambleden, once owned by the Clare family whose name is the first to appear on Magna Carta?

5) What is applied for by an MP who wishes to step down between elections?

What do you know about Buteshire?

1) Who holds the title Duke of Rothesay today?

2) What is the highest point on the Isle of Arran at 2,866 ft (874 m)?

3) Which family owned Brodick Castle (right) before it was turned over to the National Trust for Scotland?

4) Where in Buteshire would you find the smallest cathedral in Britain (below)?

5) What hard-drinking Shakespearian actor, who died two months after collapsing on stage while playing Othello at Covent Garden, owned a retreat called Woodend House on Loch Fad?

What do you know about Caernarfonshire?

1) In which town would you find
   the oldest town house in Wales,
   Aberconwy House (right)?

2) What island lies off the tip of
   the Lleyn Peninsula?

3) What political party was
   founded in Pwllheli in 1925?

4) What soldier, author and
   diplomat was born in Tremadog
   in 1888?

5) Where would you find the
   longest pier in Wales (below)?

What do you know about Caithness?

1) Before it was demolished after a fire, Thurso Castle (right) was the seat of which family?

2) What stretch of sea must you cross to get from John O'Groats to Orkney?

3) What is the most northerly castle on the British mainland?

4) What car rally used to start regularly from John O'Groats (below) before World War Two?

5) What did Sir William Alexander Smith, born in Pennyland House, near Thurso, form at the Free Church Mission Hall in Glasgow in 1883?

What do you know about Cambridgeshire?

1) Ely Cathedral's unique Octagon lantern tower (right) is the world's only medieval Gothic dome. In which century was it built?

2) In 1953, in the Cavendish Laboratory in Cambridge, James Watson and Francis Crick discovered the structure of what?

3) The last woad mill in England stood at Parson Drove near Wisbech. What colour are the flowers of the woad plant?

4) Sawston Hall (below) was rebuilt after being burned down by the Duke of Northumberland in 1553. Who was he looking for?

5) The clock chime of Great St Mary's Church in Cambridge, composed in 1793 by the Revd Dr Joseph Lowett, was adopted and made famous by which other great clock?

What do you know about Cardiganshire?

1) What holy treasure was thought to be hidden at Nanteos (right), near Aberystwyth?

2) Which two major rivers have their source on Plynlimmon?

3) Soar-y-Mynydd (below), the most remote chapel in Wales, lies near which reservoir, kept in check by Britain's tallest dam?

4) Llanddewi Brefi, where, in the 6th century, the ground rose up beneath St David so that his preaching could be seen and heard by everyone, has found new fame as the home of which *Little Britain* character?

5) Britain's longest electric cliff railway in Aberystwyth climbs up to the world's biggest what?

What do you know about Carmarthenshire?

1) Who described the Boat House at Laugharne (right) as this 'seashaken house on a breakneck of rocks'?

2) What is Llanelli's rugby team called?

3) To which hero of the Napoleonic Wars is Paxton's Tower (below) dedicated?

4) Where in Carmarthenshire did Malcolm Campbell and John Parry Thomas battle for land speed records in the 1920s?

5) What did the Romans mine at Dolaucothi?

What do you know about Cheshire?

1) What is the biggest town or city in Cheshire?

2) What television soap opera is set in Chester?

3) The Anderton Boat Lift (below), first boat lift in the world, carries boats between the Trent and Mersey Canal and which river, which flows to the docks at Runcorn?

4) What was the name of Mr Darcy's home in *Pride and Prejudice*, which was played in the 1995 BBC TV adaptation by Lyme Park (above)?

5) Which mountaineer, who was possibly the first man to climb to the top of Mount Everest, was born in Mobberley in 1886?

What do you know about Clackmannanshire?

1) Which future monarch was brought as an infant to Alloa Tower (right), the largest keep in Scotland, for safety – but, some believe, died there and was replaced by the Earl of Mar's son?

2) Who left his 'mannan' on the 'clach' in Clackmannan?

3) In what sphere did John McNabb, who founded Dollar Academy (below), make his fortune?

4) Which New World colony was founded by James VI of Scotland and Sir William Alexander of Menstrie and financed by the selling of baronetcies?

5) Ben Clach, the highest point of Clackmannanshire, is also the highest point of what range of hills?

What do you know about Cornwall?

1) Gryll's Gate in Helston (right) is a landmark on the route of what kind of dance performed in May?

2) Which novel by Rosamund Pilcher was set in St Ives?

3) What is the name of the open-air theatre (below) near Land's End, built in the 1930s by Rowena Cade, almost single-handedly?

4) What was the name of the ship wrecked off the Scilly Isles in 1967, in the world's first disaster involving an oil supertanker?

5) Which Cornish port was home to the world's first Royal Mail Packet station, set up in 1698?

What do you know about Cumberland?

1) Canon Hardwicke Drummond Rawnsley, who lived at Greta Hall (right), was a co-founder of what organisation?

2) What was the Sellafield nuclear site formerly known as?

3) Before it closed in 1998, Jefferson's Wine Merchants (below) was the oldest family-owned wine merchants in England. In which town was it?

4) Which celebrated foxhunting man from Caldbeck has a song in his honour?

5) Which Lake District writer had his ashes scattered on his favourite mountain, Haystacks, above Lake Buttermere?

What do you know about Denbighshire?

1) The entrance to which castle is guarded by a set of white painted iron gates considered to be the finest work of the Davies brothers of Bersham (right)?

2) Who was born John Rowlands in Denbigh in 1841 and went on to provide one of history's great soundbites when he met David Livingstone in Africa in 1869?

3) How do you spell the name of the longest aqueduct in Britain (below)?

4) Which James Bond actor was born in Colwyn Bay in 1946?

5) Who left for America from Rhos-on-Sea in 1170 and may have discovered the New World over 300 years before Columbus?

What do you know about Derbyshire?

1) What, at 2,088 ft (636 m), is the highest point in the Peak District, and was the site of a mass trespass in 1932?

2) Joseph Paxton built the world's largest glass house, the Great Conservatory, in the grounds of which house?

3) Chesterfield is famous for its crooked church spire (below) and as the birthplace of the minister who introduced the breathalyser test. Who was that minister?

4) Which philosopher, born in Derby in 1820, coined the phrase 'survival of the fittest'?

5) John Lombe's silk mill in Derby (below), the first silk mill in England, stands on which river?

What do you know about Devon?

1) What kind of terrier was created by a parson born in Dartmouth, home of the first castle in Britain designed specifically for artillery (right)?

2) In what year did the Pilgrim Fathers leave for America from the Mayflower Steps in Plymouth (below)?

3) Which Sherlock Holmes story is set on Dartmoor?

4) What famous hymn, reputedly played by the band on the Titanic as she sank beneath the waves, was written by Henry Francis Lyte, vicar at All Saints in Brixham, in 1847?

5) Which ancient Devon town was famous for its carpets?

What do you know about Dorset?

1) Sir Walter Raleigh rebuilt Sherborne Castle (above) as his last home in 1594. Why might a servant have poured a bucket of water over him there?

2) Of what group were George Loveless and Thomas Standfield the ringleaders?

3) What worldwide movement was founded on Brownsea Island in Poole Harbour in 1907?
BONUS QUESTION: By whom?

4) Of what Dorset stone is the Cenotaph in London made?

5) What product was promoted in a memorable TV advertisement featuring a small boy pushing his bicycle up Gold Hill in Shaftesbury (below)?

What do you know about Dumfriesshire?

1) In 1300, the 60 defenders of Caerlaverock Castle (right) held out for two days against 3,000 troops of which English king?

2) What scheme to establish a trading post in Central America was set up in 1695 by William Paterson, born near Lockerbie in 1658, and almost bankrupted Scotland?

3) In which town, boasting the narrowest hotel in Britain (below), was Air Chief Marshal 1st Lord Dowding, head of the RAF's Fighter Command during the Battle of Britain, born in 1882?

4) Which poet went along for the ride on the first steamboat journey in the world, on Dalswinton Loch in 1788?

5) Where in Dumfriesshire would you find the world's oldest post office, still in use, dating from before 1763?

What do you know about Dunbartonshire?

1) Who designed and built Hill
House in Helensburgh (right)
for Glasgow publisher
W.W. Blackie?

2) What wall ends at Old
Kilpatrick, east of Dunbarton,
on the River Clyde?

3) What make of car (below) was
manufactured at Europe's first
purpose-built car factory, in
Alexandria?

4) Which pretty village beside
Loch Lomond played the part
of 'Glendarroch' in the Scottish
television series *Take the High
Road*?

5) Which clan were outlawed by
James VI of Scotland after
slaughtering the Colquhouns in
Glen Fruin, known for ever
afterwards as the Glen of
Sorrow?

What do you know about Durham?

1) This Sanctuary knocker (right) hangs on the north entrance door of Durham Cathedral which was founded at the end of the 10th century to house the relics of which saint?

2) St Paul's Church, Jarrow (below), was dedicated in 685 and contains the oldest dedication stone in England. Which historian made the monastery at Jarrow his home for more than 50 years?

3) What did the citizens of Hartlepool hang, thinking it was a Frenchman?

4) What waterfall on the River Tees is the biggest in England in terms of water flow?

5) Which Durham town links the 'Queen of Iraq', Gertrude Bell, Roxy Music singer Bryan Ferry, and the only US state named after a president?

What do you know about East Lothian?

1) Which engineer, responsible for the Crinan Canal and the London Bridge now in Arizona, was born in 1761 at Phantassie House near Preston Mill (right), the oldest working watermill in Scotland?

2) Which conservationist, whose name is commemorated by a nearby championship golf course, was born opposite Dunbar's 17th-century Town House (below), in 1838?

3) Which landmark off the coast of East Lothian is the largest single-rock gannetry in the world?

4) Which helpful author, whose book gives us the phrase 'Heaven helps those who help themselves', was born in Haddington in 1812?

5) At what battle fought in East Lothian was Scotland's first railway, the Tranent Waggonway, used to haul cannons to the battlefield?

What do you know about Essex?

1) Tymperleys, in Colchester
(right), was the home of
William Gilbert, physician to
Elizabeth I and the first person
to coin what energetic word
from the Latin for 'like amber'?

2) Which Essex castle (below)
boasts the largest Norman arch
in the world, with a span of 28
ft (8.5 m)?

4) Name the Captain of the
Mayflower, born in Harwich
circa 1565.

5) What is the county town of
Essex?

3) Which Essex village gives its
name to a jam first produced
by Arthur Wilkin in 1885?

What do you know about Fife?

3) Of which Fife town did steel magnate Andrew Carnegie say, 'Fortunate indeed the child who first sees the light of day in that romantic town'?

4) Which two Adams were born in Kirkcaldy in the 1720s?

5) Which king died in Falkland Palace (below)?

1) Which airbase in Fife, which shares a location with Scotland's finest small Norman church (above), is the RAF's busiest fighter base and the oldest continuously operating military airfield in the world?

2) The clubhouse of which golf club overlooks Granny Clark's Wynd?

What do you know about Flintshire?

1) Where did Edward I issue a statute, in March 1284, uniting Wales and England?

2) At the summit of Moel Famau, the highest point of the Clwydian Hills, are the remains of the Jubilee Tower (below), the first monument in Britain built in the Egyptian style, erected in 1809 to commemorate the Golden Jubilee of which monarch?

3) Whose well can be found at Holywell (below)?

4) What seminal work of Bishop William Morgan, who is buried in St Asaph Cathedral, was used at Prince Charles's Investiture as Prince of Wales in 1969?

5) Who threw a punch in Rhyl during the 2001 General Election campaign?

What do you know about Glamorgan?

1) When Dr William Price of Llantrisant died in 1893 at the age of 93, three years after becoming a father by his housekeeper, he became the first person in Britain to be publicly what?

2) To where did Tom Jones return in May 2005 to give a concert marking 65 years since he was born there?

3) Which newspaper tycoon bought St Donat's Castle (below) in 1925 and turned it into a Hollywood-style fantasy for his mistress, actress Marion Davies?

4) At Margam there is a magnificent Norman church (above), a 'Gothick' castle and the world's longest what?

5) Which seaside resort, home to one of the world's first passenger railways, gets its name from the French word for breasts?

What do you know about Gloucestershire?

1) Who began to translate the Bible into English while tutoring at Little Sodbury Manor (right)?

2) Who did Daniel Defoe meet at the Llandoger Trow in Bristol (below) and later turn into Robinson Crusoe?

3) What kind of cheese do they chase down Cooper's Hill in May?

4) What kind of school did Robert Raikes, born in Gloucester in 1735, initiate?

5) What was the name of the ship in which John and Sebastian Cabot sailed from Bristol to Newfoundland in 1497?

What do you know about Hampshire?

1) Where in Hampshire was the first Burberry shop?

2) Which monarch was imprisoned at Carisbrooke Castle on the Isle of Wight and tried to escape by climbing out of a window?

3) In 1876 Rector's wife Mary Sumner organised the first-ever meeting of what group, in the Rectory at Old Arlesford (below)?

4) Which author was born at 393 Old Commercial Road, Portsmouth (below), in 1812?

5) In 1974 the Postmaster General, born in Southampton in 1925, disappeared off a beach in Miami and was assumed drowned, until he turned up alive and well and living with his secretary in Australia. What was his name? BONUS QUESTION: And what was the name of his secretary?

What do you know about the Hebrides?

1) On which Hebridean island would you find the Round Church (right), built in 1797?

2) Who rowed 'Betty Burke' from Benbecula to Skye in 1746?

3) Who finished writing his last book at Barnhill on Jura (below) in 1948?

4) On which island is Stornoway?

5) Where would you find the Old Man of Storr?

What do you know about Herefordshire?

1) What name did Alexander Pope give to John Kyrle, who lived at Kyrle House (right)?

2) Which river does Symonds Yat overlook?

3) What celebrated treasure was created by the Prebend of Hereford, Richard di Bello, in 1289?

5) Of what kind of library does Hereford Cathedral (below) possess the largest in the world?

4) Which poet, born in Ledbury in 1332, wrote *Piers Plowman*?

What do you know about Hertfordshire?

1) What did Lieutenant William Leefe Robinson shoot down over Hertfordshire in 1916 and win a Victoria Cross for so doing?

2) Lady Katherine Ferrers, owner of Markyate Cell (below), lived a double life as lady of the house by day and lady of the road by night – how did she become known?

3) Who emerged naked from a soup tureen and danced on the table for her husband's birthday party at Brocket Hall (below)?

4) Jane Wenham of Walkern was the last person to be sentenced to death for being a what, in 1711?

5) A 200 ft (61 m) tall monument to the Duke of Bridgewater, original owner of Ashridge House, overlooks Aldbury – he gave his name to the first modern example of a what?

What do you know about Huntingdonshire?

1) Whose old grammar school in Huntingdon (below) is now a museum of his life?

2) Which car maker, who started life as a newspaper delivery boy for W.H. Smith, was born in Alwalton in 1863 and was buried in the church there in 1933?

3) What was the Christian name of the landscape gardener 'Capability' Brown, buried in Fenstanton in 1783?

4) Who was sent under house arrest to Kimbolton Castle in 1534 and died there two years later in 1536?

5) Which poet was inspired by the beauty and solitude of Little Gidding (below) to call the last of the poems in his *Four Quartets* 'Little Gidding'?

What do you know about Inverness-shire?

1) In what BBC television series did Ardverikie Castle (right) star?

2) Who lived in paradise with an otter called Edal at 'Camusfearna' on the Sound of Sleat?

3) Leanach Cottage (below) stands in the middle of which battlefield, where the last pitched battle on British soil was fought?

4) What Bloomsbury group artist, and lover of economist John Maynard Keynes, was born in Inverness in 1885?

5) In the Second World War, Achnacarry Castle, ancestral home of Clan Cameron, was headquarters for those training to wear what headwear?

What do you know about Kent?

1) The Saxon font at St Martin's Church in Canterbury (above) is said to be based on the one at which Ethelbert of Kent, the first Saxon king to be converted to Christianity, was baptised – by whom was he baptised?

2) Which architect, who designed the clock faces of Big Ben, was buried in Ramsgate in 1852?

3) Which river divides the Men of Kent from Kentish Men?

4) Which Kent castle hosted the four knights who murdered Archbishop Thomas à Becket on the night before their dreadful deed, and was also the childhood home of journalist Bill Deedes, recipient of the 'Dear Bill' letters, and later the home of Kenneth Clark, presenter of the television series *Civilisation*?

5) Walter Arnold, manufacturer of the Arnold Motor Carriage (below), the first petrol-driven car to be manufactured and sold in England, was the first person to be convicted of what outrage?

What do you know about Kincardineshire?

1) John Arbuthnot of Arbuthnot, early spin doctor and author of the pamphlet *The Art of Political Lying*, created what figure in 1712 who, while designed to represent the whole United Kingdom, became the personification of England?

2) The Thomson Steam Omnibus (below) was but one of the achievements of Robert William Thomson, born in Stonehaven. What did he patent some 40 years before the person most commonly credited with its invention?

3) Dunnottar (below) was the last castle in Scotland to hold out against whom?

4) What kind of bag would you have expected to find in the entrance hall at Fasque, before it was sold in 2008?

5) Civil engineer Richard Henry Brunton, born in Muchalls in 1841, is celebrated in which country for establishing its lighthouse service?

What do you know about Kinross-shire?

1) When looking out from Kinross House (right), Scotland's first great classical country house, which castle is framed by the elaborate Fish Gate?

2) Which river is crossed by the double bridge at Rumbling Bridge (below)?

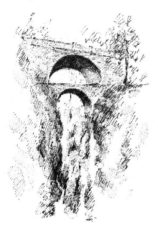

3) Scotland's largest outdoor rock festival, held annually in July on a disused airfield at Balado, is called what?

4) Who turned Blair Crambeth into Blairadam?

5) Who was held prisoner for 11 months in the answer to question one?

What do you know about Kirkcudbrightshire?

1) Buried in a silver casket beside his wife at New Abbey (below) is the 'sweet heart' of the founder of which Oxford College?

4) Which Scotsman, born in a gamekeeper's cottage near Kirkbean in 1747, became the 'Father of the American Navy'?

2) Scotland's second oldest lighthouse at Southerness Point (right) was built in 1749 to guide ships entering the estuary of which river?

3) What is the name of the highest peak in southern Scotland?

5) Glenlair, near Castle Douglas, was the home of which great scientist, of whom Albert Einstein said, 'One scientific epoch ended and another began with . . .'?

What do you know about Lanarkshire?

1) What did Cadzow become in 1445?

2) Robert Stevenson, born in Glasgow in 1772, established a dynasty for building what?

3) The Hamilton Mausoleum (below) has the longest and deepest what of any building in Europe?

4) On which Glasgow street would you find the Tolbooth Steeple (below)?

5) What is the tallest free-standing structure in Scotland and the only one in the world able to turn through 360 degrees from the ground up?

What do you know about Lancashire?

1) On what favourite piece of meat did James I bestow a knighthood at Hoghton Tower (right) in 1617?

2) What was Mancunian John Alcock the first to do (along with Arthur Brown)?

3) The largest clock faces in England crown which Lancashire landmark (below)?

4) What two spinning aids to weaving were invented in Lancashire in the 18th century? BONUS QUESTION: Who invented them?

5) From where in Lancashire in 1652 did George Fox see 'a great multitude waiting to be gathered in by God' – the vision which inspired him to found the Society of Friends?

What do you know about Leicestershire?

1) The first-ever broadcast of bell music came from the Carillon and War Memorial Tower (right) in which town?

2) What did Sue Townsend set in Leicester?

3) Whose home is Belvoir Castle (below)?

4) Lord Chancellor 'Derry' Irvine famously compared himself to which historic figure, who died and was buried in Leicester?

5) Which town did the 3rd Marquess of Waterford and his hunting pals paint red?

What do you know about Lincolnshire?

1) England's oldest bridge with
houses on it, Lincoln High
Bridge (right), carries Lincoln
High Street across which river?

2) What kind of fingers were first
produced in Grimsby in 1955?

3) Which church did the brothers
born at Epworth Rectory
(below) found?

4) Who asked 'Maud' to 'come
into the garden' at Harrington
Hall, near Spilsby?

5) Which Lincolnshire town has
the highest church spire in
England?

What do you know about Merioneth?

1) What play did Noël Coward write while staying at Portmeirion (right) in 1941?

2) Where in Merioneth would you go to catch a Gwyniad?

3) During the Wars of the Roses the 'Men of Harlech' Castle (below) held out under siege for seven years. Were they Lancastrians or Yorkists?

4) What is the distinction of Dinas Oleu, a gorse-covered hill above Barmouth?

5) Nonconformist preacher Michael Jones of Bala was the inspiration behind the founding of an independent Welsh community in which region of South America?

What do you know about Middlesex?

1) What Armistice Day tradition was thought up by Australian reporter Edward Honey, buried at Northwood?

2) In 1827 Bruce Castle (right) was bought by Sir Rowland Hill to run as a progressive school – it now houses a museum about what service that Hill went on to reform and develop?

3) Which satirical artist gave his name to a roundabout, built long after his death near to the house where he used to spend the summer (below)?

4) Who built a huge house near Twickenham that gave its name to a style of architecture? BONUS QUESTION: What was the house called?

5) What did Zephaniah Holwell, buried in the church of St John the Baptist in Pinner, survive in 1756?

What do you know about Midlothian?

1) What did William Smellie edit, and produce the first volumes of, at his shop in Anchor Place, off the Royal Mile in Edinburgh?

2) Which king was born in Edinburgh Castle in 1566?

3) John Knox's House (below) gazes up the road at which kirk?

4) What mathematical method of calculation did John Napier, Laird of Merchiston Castle, discover?

5) Where in Midlothian would you find the Prentice Pillar (below)?

What do you know about Monmouthshire?

1) Who wrote the following words above Tintern Abbey (right)?

'For I have learned
To look on nature, not as in
    the hour
of thoughtless youth; but
    hearing often times
The still, sad music of
    humanity . . .'

2) Newport can boast one of only two transporter bridges in Britain (below). Which river, with a tidal range greater than any other river in Britain, does it transport traffic across?

3) What is the modern name for Isca Silurum, the only Roman legionary fort in Wales?

4) With what oriental technique for creating a hard lacquer did Pontypool become prominent in the 18th century?

5) What is the great legacy of Aneurin Bevan, born in Tredegar in 1897?

What do you know about Montgomeryshire?

1) The descendants of which empire-builder once owned Powis Castle (right)?

2) In which town was the last native Welsh parliament held, in 1404?

3) Which town is at the exact centre of Wales and boasts the only remaining market hall of its kind in Wales (below)?

4) The ancestors of which banking family built the Dolobran Meeting House in 1701, the first Quaker meeting house in Wales?

5) Whom did Sir Pryce Pryce-Jones use for the first-ever celebrity endorsement of his mail order business, the world's first, which he ran from Newtown?

What do you know about Morayshire?

1) 'Dull is the eye that will not
weep to see,
Thy walls defaced, thy
mouldering shrines removed,
By British hands, which it had
best behoved
To guard those relics ne'er to
be restored.'

To what was Lord Byron
referring in these lines?

2) What is the county town of
Morayshire?

3) What village was moved to
make way for Gordon Castle
(below)?

4) What town, near where King
Duncan and three witches held
court, can boast both the first
monument in Britain to
commemorate Nelson's victory
at Trafalgar and Sueno's Stone
(below), Scotland's tallest
Pictish stone?

5) Where did Peter and Eileen
Caddy go in 1964 to establish
an alternative way of life?

What do you know about Nairnshire?

1) 'All ye tourists who want to be
   away,
   From the crowded city for a
   brief holiday
   The town of Nairn is worth a
   visit, I do confess,
   And it's only about fifteen
   miles from Inverness.'

   Who wrote these lines about
   Nairn?

2) Cawdor Castle was built in the
   late 14th century around what
   was thought to be a hawthorn
   tree (below). What kind of tree
   has it turned out to be?

3) What was the name of the
   family who originally built
   Cawdor Castle (above)?

4) Culbin Forest is home to the
   largest game bird in Britain –
   what bird is that?

5) William Whitelaw, born in
   Nairn in 1918, became whose
   deputy?

What do you know about Norfolk?

1) A statue of which explorer, who gave his name to a Canadian city and island, stands outside the Custom House at King's Lynn (right)?

2) Who was born at Park House, Sandringham, in 1961?

3) In which Norfolk village was Lord Nelson (below) born in 1758?

4) By which part of the anatomy can you distinguish a Norfolk terrier from a Norwich terrier?

5) William Coke of Holkham Hall was the first man to wear what kind of hat?

What do you know about Northamptonshire?

1) Who built the Triangular Lodge (right) in the grounds of Rushton Hall?

2) Where was Mary, Queen of Scots first buried after she had been executed at Fotheringay in 1587?

3) Who designed the family seat (below) of the baron who sponsored the car in which James Hunt won his first Grand Prix in 1975? BONUS QUESTION: Name the baron and the house.

4) What did Sir Robert Watson-Watt pioneer from the back of a Morris van near Daventry in 1935?

5) Who featured in the First World War recruiting poster designed by *Punch* illustrator Alfred Leete, born in Achurch in 1882?

What do you know about Northumberland?

1) Cragside (right), the first house in the world to be lit by electricity, was the home of engineer Sir William Armstrong. What castle did he later buy?

2) Who was the first Bishop of Lindisfarne?

3) Which engineer, buried in Kirkwhelpington, built *Turbinia*, the world's first steam turbine-driven boat (below)?

4) Where in Northumberland would you find a famous herd of white cattle, a bull from which was the subject of an engraving by Thomas Bewick in 1789?

5) Which World Cup-winning brothers were born in Ashington?

What do you know about Nottinghamshire?

1) The 16-ton bell with the deepest tone of any bell in England, which hangs in the Nottingham Council House (right), takes its name from what giant right-hand man?

2) Which shop did the first Lord Trent found?

3) Which Pilgrim Father, ancestor of Bing Crosby and Richard Gere, amongst others, was born in Scrooby in 1567?

5) Which Nottinghamshire village was immortalised by Washington Irving, who applied its name to his home town of New York?

4) How did Thomas Cranmer (below) born in Aslockton in 1489, die?

What do you know about Orkney?

1) What is the name of the oldest known prehistoric village in Europe, which can be found on the west coast of Mainland, Orkney (right)?

2) To whom is the cathedral at Kirkwall dedicated?

3) What nationality of prisoner built a chapel out of two Nissen huts (below) on Lamb Holm during the Second World War?

4) Which King of Scotland gained Orkney and Shetland as part of his dowry?

5) The parents of which writer, the author of *Rip Van Winkle* and *The Legend of Sleepy Hollow*, emigrated to New York from Orkney in the 18th century?

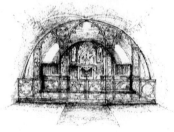

What do you know about Oxfordshire?

1) Who used to row down the river with his muse from Folly Bridge, to picnic at Godstow, where Henry II's 'Fair Rosamund' is buried?

2) Alice, the Duchess of Suffolk, who rests in a magnificent tomb in St Mary's Church in Ewelme (right), was whose granddaughter?

3) Name the three Oxford martyrs commemorated by Sir George Gilbert Scott's Martyrs Memorial (below).

4) What is the River Thames sometimes called as it runs through Oxford?

5) For which Oxford museum – established in 1678 as the first public museum in the world – was the word 'museum' invented?

What do you know about Peeblesshire?

1) What was the formal title of 'Old Q', born in Peebles in 1724?

2) The publishers of which dictionary were also born in Peebles (right)?

3) The Bear Gates (below), which closed behind Bonnie Prince Charlie in 1745, and will remain shut until a Stuart king is crowned in London, guard which house?

4) Margot Tennant, born on her family's estate of Glen, near Peebles, in 1864, went on to marry which prime minister?

5) What is the 1st Lord Tweedsmuir's most celebrated novel?

What do you know about Pembrokeshire?

1) The Tudor Merchant's House in Tenby (right) stands close to the largest parish church in Wales, where there is a memorial to mathematician Robert Recorde, born in the town in 1510. Which mathematical sign did he invent?

2) Pentre Ifan (below) is constructed of the same bluestones from the Preseli Hills as which other ancient monument?

3) What name do the cave below Pembroke Castle and a popular Irish broadcaster share?

4) The Teifi was the last river in Britain where what creatures were seen?

5) Lucy Walter, born in Roch Castle around 1630, was the mother of which of Charles II's children?

What do you know about Perthshire?

1) What was the ecclesiastical
capital of Scotland prior to St
Andrews?

2) Which castle was subject to the
last ever siege of a castle in
Britain, in 1746?

3) The smallest listed building in
Europe (below) was put up in
Comrie in 1874 to study what?

4) Where did Charles II walk
along Scotland's longest room
(above) to the last coronation
in Scotland, in 1651?

5) Which uncle and nephew
acting duo were born in Crieff
in 1947 and 1971 respectively?

What do you know about Radnorshire?

1) Clyro Court (right), home of Sir Thomas Baskerville, where Sir Arthur Conan Doyle stayed while writing *The Hound of the Baskervilles*, overlooks the village that found fame in whose lyrical diaries?

2) Old Radnor Church, home to a matchless 16th-century organ case (below), the oldest of its kind in Britain, is the only church in Wales dedicated to which saint, who features in the carol 'Good King Wenceslas'?

3) Which 'Father' of the Industrial Revolution retired to Doldowlod Hall, near Rhayader, in 1785?

4) In 1904 Nantgwyllt House was drowned beneath the waters of the new Caban Coch reservoir. Which poet and his child bride had lived there briefly in 1812, before they both separately died by drowning in later life?

5) What is Britain's longest archaeological monument, stretching 149 miles (240 km) from Chepstow to Prestatyn?

What do you know about Renfrewshire?

1) Which son of Greenock (right) is commemorated on light bulbs across the world?

2) The family of which US president's wife emigrated to America from Paisley?

3) The daughter of Robert the Bruce, Princess Marjorie, who is buried in Paisley Abbey (below), is the mother of what royal dynasty?

4) Who landed in a field near Eaglesham in 1941 with 'an important message for the Duke of Hamilton'?

5) What service, the oldest of its kind in the world, was established at Renfrew in 1933 when Jimmy Orwell flew to Islay to help a fisherman with acute peritonitis?

What do you know about Ross and Cromarty?

1) Which distillery can be found just outside Tain, Scotland's oldest royal burgh?

2) Which football club is owned by the present owner of the Balnagowan estate, once the home of the Clan Ross?

3) Buried inside the East Church at Cromarty (below) is Sir Thomas Urquart, who wrote a work called *Logopandecteision* in which he proposed the introduction of a universal what?

4) The National Memorial (above) was erected above Dingwall in 1907 in memory of Major-General Sir Hector Macdonald, known as 'Fighting Mac', who appears on the label of which drink?

5) What is the name of the small island off Wester Ross that was bombarded with anthrax by scientists from Porton Down in 1942?

What do you know about Roxburghshire?

1) Whose heart is said to be buried at Melrose Abbey (right)?

2) Jeddart hand-ba, now played with footballs, was originally played with what?

3) The remains of what royal burgh lie within the grounds of Floors Castle (below)?

4) What is unusual about the staircase at Ferniehurst Castle, ancestral home of the Kerrs?

5) Who was born in Hawick in 1940 and became the first man to sail single-handed around the world the wrong way?

What do you know about Rutland?

1) Hanging in Oakham Castle (right) is a unique collection of what?

2) What is the family name of the Duke of Rutland?

3) What was the favourite colour of the earl who introduced the Lonsdale Belt in boxing (below)?

4) Which native of Rutland raised fears of a 'Popish plot' against Charles II?

5) Comic actor and presenter Stephen Fry, celebrity chef Rick Stein and film director John Schlesinger are all alumni of which school?

What do you know about Selkirkshire?

1) Items belonging to which literary Sheriff of Selkirk are on display at Selkirk Courthouse (right)?

2) The 1st Duke of Buccleuch was also the only Duke of what?

3) Galashiels (below) is famed for what kind of material which gets its name, not from a nearby river, but from a misspelling?

4) Which African explorer, born in Foulshiels in 1771, was the first European to see the River Niger?

5) What is Selkirk Bannock?

What do you know about Shetland?

1) Symbister House (right), built by Robert Bruce of Symbister and the finest Georgian house in Shetland, can be found on which island?

2) What is the family name of the Marquess of Zetland?

3) Scalloway (below) was capital of Shetland until it was replaced in 1708 by where?

4) What company did Arthur Anderson, born in the Bod of Gremista on Shetland in 1792, co-found?

5) What politician, born in Shetland in 1942, is not fondly remembered for claiming, 'Je ne regrette rien'?

What do you know about Shropshire?

1) Who was born at The Mount, in Shrewsbury (right), in 1809?

2) What popular pub name stands in the grounds of Boscobel House?

3) Which Shropshire town has a leaning tower with a slant three times that of the Leaning Tower of Pisa (below) and the only inland cliff railway in England?

4) What was the name of the Shropshire man who became the longest-living Englishman of all time, reaching the age of 152?

5) In which Shropshire town did Dr William Penny Brookes institute a series of games 'for the promotion of moral, physical and intellectual improvement' which led to the founding of the modern Olympics?

What do you know about Somerset?

1) Which fictional character was married in the 15th-century church at Oare (right), where her creator's grandfather had been vicar?

2) Whose staff, when stuck in the ground at Wearyall Hill, blossomed into the Glastonbury Thorn?

3) As well as a kind of chair (below), Bath is known for a bun and what brand of biscuit, invented to take away the bitter taste of the spa water?

4) Where in Somerset would you find the Vicar's Close, the oldest unchanged English street in existence?

5) Somerset can boast the oldest bridge in England, Tarr Steps on Exmoor, and the oldest known roadway in the world, on the Somerset Levels – what is that roadway called?

What do you know about Staffordshire?

1) What was then the biggest anchor in the world (below) was made in Netherton by Noah Hingley and Sons for the ship captained by Edward Smith, born in Stoke-on-Trent in 1850. What ship was that?

2) Which river flows past the little Fishing Temple in Beresford Dale (right) built in 1674 by Charles Cotton, where he and his friend Izaak Walton would spend many a happy hour?

3) Apart from Josiah Wedgwood, who was the other Josiah who helped transform Stoke-on-Trent into the pottery capital of the world in the 18th century?

4) Button Gwinnett's signature, found on documents belonging to Wolverhampton's Bluecoat School, is one of the most valuable signatures in the world because he signed what other document?

5) Edward Wightman, put to death in the market square at Lichfield in 1612, was the last person in England to be burned for what?

What do you know about Stirlingshire?

1) In 1548 Mary, Queen of Scots, planted five trees in the grounds of Callendar House (right) in Falkirk to commemorate her friendship with the 'four Marys' who accompanied her to France as an infant. Which Mary lived at Callendar?

2) Who gave the sermon at the coronation of James VI in Stirling's Church of the Holy Rood?

3) The Wallace Monument (below) is sited where William Wallace watched the English army before which battle in 1297?

4) Which Falkirk ironworks produced the world's first iron plough, Henry Shrapnel's shells, James Watt's first steam engine and the carronades used against the French in the Napoleonic Wars?

5) Explorer James Bruce of Kinnaird House was the first man to verify the source of what river?

What do you know about Suffolk?

1) Who made famous Willy Lott's Cottage (right)?

2) Which son of Suffolk translated *The Rubaiyat of Omar Khayyam* into English?

3) England's oldest folly, Freston's Tower (above), sits beside which river?

4) Where in Suffolk would you find the Rowley Mile, at 2½ miles (4 km) long and 176 ft (54 m) wide the longest and widest horse-racing straight in the world?

5) Admiral Edward Vernon, known as 'Old Grog' from his coat made of grogram, a mix of silk and mohair, introduced into the Royal Navy a daily ration of what, which has ever since been called 'grog'?

What do you know about Surrey?

1) In which town was Britain's oldest mosque, the Shah Jehan Mosque (right), opened in 1889?

2) Which theatrical peer was born in Dorking in 1907?

3) Watts Chapel in Compton (below) was built by artist G.F. Watts's second wife Mary. Who was his first wife?

4) Where did the Surrey Iron Railway, opened in 1803 as the world's first public railway, meet the River Thames?

5) William Oughtred, rector of Albury in the 17th century, was a noted mathematician. What mathematical sign did he introduce?

What do you know about Sussex?

1) Enid Bagnold, buried in Rottingdean, is the author of which equine novel?

2) The young daughter of which king is buried in the church at Bosham?

3) Who were the two architects commissioned by the Prince Regent to turn his seaside farmhouse into Brighton Pavilion (below)?

4) Emma Hart, who danced naked on the table at Uppark (below) for the delectation of Sir Harry Fetherstonhaugh and his friends, went on to become the wife of whom? BONUS QUESTION: And whose mistress?

5) 'Away to sweet Felpham, for heaven is there,' said William Blake. While living in Felpham he wrote the words to 'Jerusalem' as the preface to his long poem *Milton*. Who put 'Jerusalem' to music?

What do you know about Sutherland?

1) Who lived at Dunrobin Castle (right) and is commemorated by a huge statue on Beinn a' Bhragaidh, overlooking Golspie?

2) What bank was founded by Thomas Sutherland?

3) Who built the present Skibo Castle (below), where Madonna married Guy Ritchie in December 2000?

4) Varrich Castle, which lies in the shadow of Ben Hope and Ben Loyal, is the spiritual home of which clan?

5) What is the name of the cave, with the largest entrance of any sea cave in Britain, that lies beneath Durness, mainland Britain's most north-westerly village?

What do you know about Warwickshire?

1) What did Parson Francis Gastrell cut down in the garden of Shakespeare's former home, New Place, prior to burning the house down and being run out of town?

2) What intellectual society used to meet one Monday evening every month at Soho House (below) in Handsworth?

3) Who designed Birmingham Town Hall (below)?

4) Who was Peeping Tom peeping at and where?

5) Triumph motorcycles were once made in which village, reckoned to be the geographical centre of England?

What do you know about West Lothian?

1) What is the family name of the earls who have a private pew in Dalmeny Church (right), Scotland's finest Romanesque church?

2) What is Scotland's biggest listed structure?

3) The House of the Binns (below), the first house to be acquired by the National Trust for Scotland under the country houses scheme, is the ancestral home of which outspoken former MP?

4) What is the county town of West Lothian?

5) What village, which gives its name to an Irish Duke, lies at the gates of Scotland's largest house, Hopetoun House?

What do you know about Westmorland?

1) The Bridge House at Ambleside (right) was built astride the river in order to avoid what, allegedly?

2) On which mountain would you be striding along Striding Edge?

3) In the grounds of Levens Hall (below) you can find the oldest and most extensive example of what type of garden feature?

4) On which lake did racing driver Sir Henry Segrave lose his life in 1930 while trying to set a new world water speed record?

5) Which one of Henry VIII's wives was born in Kendal Castle?

What do you know about Wigtownshire?

1) Fergus, Lord of Galloway, built Whithorn Priory (right) in the 12th century on the site of Scotland's first stone church, built in the 5th century by whom?

2) Explorer Sir John Ross, born near Stranraer (below) in 1777, named the northernmost point of the American mainland Boothia Peninsula in honour of his sponsor Sir Felix Booth. What had made Booth his fortune?

3) Where would you find the biggest second-hand bookshop in Scotland?

4) Who wrote a book about his childhood home in Monreith, entitled *The House of Elrig*?

5) The final scenes of which cult 1974 film starring Edward Woodward were filmed on the cliffs south of the Isle of Whithorn?

What do you know about Wiltshire?

1) Who is said to have aligned Box Tunnel, the longest railway tunnel in the world when it was completed in 1837, so that the sun would shine right through it at dawn on his birthday, April 9th, every year?

2) What did Joseph Priestley discover in his laboratory at Bowood House in 1775?

3) In the churchyard of Malmesbury Abbey (below) lies Hannah Twynnoy, a barmaid at the White Lion Inn who died in 1703, the last person in England to die by what means?

4) The oriel window (above) of which abbey is the subject of the world's oldest photograph, taken by William Fox Talbot in 1835?

5) What suave author is buried beneath an obelisk in the quiet village churchyard at Sevenhampton near Swindon, along with his wife Ann and son Caspar?

What do you know about Worcestershire?

1) What writer's friend is buried, interred, laid to rest, entombed or consigned in the churchyard of St James's at West Malvern?

2) Which native of Worcestershire featured on the Bank of England's £20 note from 1999 until 2007?

3) What great English novel was inspired by the Lygon family of Madresfield (below)?

4) Harvington Hall near Kidderminster (above) possesses a number of the finest examples of Nicholas Owen's work. What was he renowned for building?

5) What make of car from Worcestershire is the only car ever to have been displayed in the window of Harrods?

What do you know about Yorkshire?

1) Richmond Castle (right), with the oldest original castle walls in Britain, towers above which river?

2) Which Yorkshire town was in 1914 the first in England to come under German fire, when the town's Grand Hotel (below) was badly damaged by shell fire from four German cruisers?

3) Whose toffee was first produced in Halifax?

4) What explosive revolutionary was born in York in 1570?

5) The world's longest-running television situation comedy, *Last of the Summer Wine*, is largely filmed in and around which Yorkshire town?

Answers

General Knowledge

Page 3

1) South Downs National Park
2) Hawthorn Tree
3) Robert the Bruce
4) River Severn
5) Swan
6) Chelmsford
7) Cornish
8) Derbyshire
9) Holy or Holyhead Island
10) Orkney

Page 4

1) St Davids, Pembrokeshire
2) Only stamps not to include the country of origin (since they were the first and, for a while, the only stamps in the world)
3) Graham Sutherland
4) Dolgellau
5) To The Manor Born
6) Fraserburgh
7) Blenheim Palace (Duke of Marlborough)
8) River Stour or Great Stour
9) Adam Smith (Wealth of Nations)
10) Morris Minor

Page 5

1) Nell Gwyn
2) Wanlockhead, Dumfriesshire 1531ft (467m)
   Bonus: Leadhills, Lanarkshire 1295ft (395m)
3) Fotheringay Castle, Northants
4) Faversham, Kent
5) MG
6) Charles Rennie Mackintosh
7) Stevenage, Herts (Lewis Hamilton was born there, Barbara Follett is MP for Stevenage)
8) Clapham Junction
9) Wigtownshire
10) Carmarthen

ANSWERS

Page 6

1) Mother Shipton
2) Elgin Cathedral
3) Bicycles
4) John Locke
5) 58
6) Inverness (Town House)
7) Northamptonshire
8) Flint
9) Henry V
10) Irn Bru

Page 7

1) Hertfordshire (Hartford, Connecticut)
2) Louth, Lincolnshire
3) Campbell
   Bonus: Cameron
4) Derbyshire
5) Llandudno, Caernarfonshire
6) Dick Turpin
7) Durham Cathedral
8) Sooty
9) Colonel David Stirling
10) Brecon Beacons National Park

Page 8

1) George Eliot
2) Skye Terrier
3) Arnold (Matthew Arnold and Malcolm Arnold)
4) Holyhead

5) Eric Morecambe
6) Mini
7) 1973 (Other victories were in 1974 and 1977)
8) Queen Elizabeth I
9) Herefordshire
10) James Boswell

Page 9

1) York
2) An acre
3) The Skull and Crossbones or Jolly Roger
4) Southend-On-Sea, Essex
5) Wigtown
6) Good
7) Jim Clark, Sir Jackie Stewart
8) Lutine Bell
9) Lyle's Golden Syrup
10) Anglesey

Page 10

1) Isle of Skye
2) ICI
3) Austin
4) Yorkshire
5) Blaenavon
6) Malcolm
7) Radnorshire
8) Scapa Flow, Orkney
9) Japan
10) 11 (Eleven) (Edward the Elder, Edward the Martyr, Edward the Confessor and Edward I to VIII)

Page 11 – Multiple Choice

1) A – A cricket ball
2) C – Declaration of Arbroath
3) B – Joseph Arch
4) C – Stephen Langton
5) C – Pedal bicycle
6) A – Abbots Bromley horn dance
7) B – Knighton
8) A – E
9) B – William Cobbett

Page 12 – Multiple Choice

10) C – Abercorn
11) C – Pembroke Dock
12) B – Forth Railway Bridge
13) A – Ben Hope
14) C – Coniston Water
15) B – Water closet
16) C – Charles Darwin (Erasmus Darwin and Josiah Wedgwood)
17) B – York Minster
18) C – C.P. Snow
19) C – Flodden
20) B – A church tower

Page 13 – Odd One Out

1) D – Sir John Betjeman
2) B – Steam turbine (Invented by Charles Parsons)
   *A – Pneumatic tyre invented by Robert Thomson of Kincardineshire
   C – Adhesive postage stamp invented by James Chalmers of Arbroath, Angus.
   D – Hypnosis invented by James Braid from Fife*
3) A – Once in Royal David's City (Written by Dublin-born Mrs Cecil Frances Alexander)
   *B – Amazing Grace written by John Newton
   C – Jerusalem written by William Blake
   D – Rock of Ages written by Augustus Toplady*
4) A – Cliveden House
   *B – Hawarden Castle – William Gladstone
   C – Dalmeny – Earl of Rosebery
   D – Hughenden Manor – Benjamin Disraeli*
5) D – Lloyds Insurance
6) C – Guildford Cathedral (*designed by Sir Edward Maufe*)
   *A – red telephone box designed by Giles Gilbert Scott
   B – Albert Memorial designed by George Gilbert Scott
   D – Shakespeare Memorial Theatre, Stratford designed by Elisabeth Scott*

Page 14 – Odd One Out

7) B – Sir Walter Scott
8) D – Ralph Vaughan Williams (born in Gloucestershire)
9) D – Lytton Strachey (ashes given to family or friends)
10) C – Oasis (from Manchester)
11) A – Queen Victoria (buried in the Royal Mausoleum at Frogmore)
12) A – Colchester (county town of Essex is Chelmsford)
B – Dorchester is county town of Dorset
C – Oakham is county town of Rutland
D – Reading is county town of Berkshire
13) B – Exeter
14) C – Herefordshire Beacon (Worcestershire Beacon, 1395 ft, 425m, is the highest point of the Malvern Hills)
A – Cleeve Hill is the highest point of the Cotswolds
B – Scafell Pike is the highest point in England
D – Brown Willy is the highest point on Bodmin Moor in Cornwall
15) A – Ashbourne, Derbyshire

Page 15 – Odd One Out

16) A – Neil Munro (born Inveraray)
17) D – Co-operative Bank (founded in Manchester)
A – Barclays founded by Barclay family from Kincardineshire
B – HSBC founded by Thomas Sutherland from Aberdeenshire
C – Coutts founded by Thomas Coutts from Edinburgh
18) C – The Merrick (2766ft 843m – a Munro is a Scottish mountain over 3000ft)
A – Lochnagar is 3790ft (1155m)
B – Ben Hope is 3041ft (927m)
D – Ben Macdhui is 4295ft (1309m)
19) C – Berwick-on-Tweed
A – Dingwall is the county town of Ross & Cromarty
B – Dornoch is the county town of Sutherland
D – Jedburgh is the county town of Roxburghshire
20) D – Kinross House (designed by Sir William Bruce)
21) B – Henry Tudor – (as Henry VII he is buried in Westminster Abbey)

22) B – Edward III (born Windsor Castle)
A – Henry VII was born in Pembroke Castle
C – Edward II was born in Caernarfon Castle
D – Henry V was born in Monmouth

26) C – Edward VIII (never crowned)
27) B – Peterborough (lies on the River Nene)
28) C – Rye (is an ancient town)
29) D – William Gladstone (educated at Eton)
30) A – Stirling Moss

Page 16 – Odd One Out

23) C – Helvellyn (Lake District)
24) B – Machynlleth
A – Montgomery is the county town of Montgomeryshire
C – Beaumaris is the county town of Anglesey
D – Presteigne is the county town of Radnorshire
25) D – William Gladstone (born in Liverpool)
A – Geoffrey Howe was born in Port Talbot
B – Michael Heseltine was born in Swansea
C – John Prescott was born in Prestatyn

Page 17 – The One And Only

1) Mount Snowdon
2) Cape Cornwall
3) Coldstream Guards
4) Bassenthwaite Lake
5) Revd John Witherspoon
6) Thomas Gainsborough's (in Sudbury, Suffolk)
7) Montgomeryshire
8) Coventry
9) Elvis Presley
10) St David of Wales (St Andrew of Scotland was a disciple and St George was a Roman Turk)
11) Lichfield Cathedral
12) The Duke Of Atholl
Bonus: Queen Victoria
13) Llanelli, Carmarthenshire

Page 18 – The One And Only

14) Bill Deedes (In Harold Macmillan's cabinet as Minister without Portfolio and Minister for Information, and Editor of the *Daily Telegraph*)
15) Palindrome
16) Devon
17) Cardinal Beaton
18) Only round tower house in Scotland
19) Berwick-on-Tweed
20) Beaumaris, Anglesey
21) Dumfriesshire (Caerlaverock Castle)
22) Maldon, Essex
23) Welshpool, Montgomeryshire

Page 19 – The One And Only

24) Sompting, Sussex
25) Monmouth

Page 20 – There's More Than One?

1) Cambridge
   Northampton
   Temple Church, London
   Little Maplestead, Essex
2) Northumbria
   Mercia
   East Anglia
   Essex
   Kent
   Sussex
   Wessex
3) 5th Earl of Lonsdale
   Winston Churchill
4) Bangor
   Cardiff
   Newport
   St Davids
   Swansea
5) Marlborough, Wiltshire
   Stockton-On-Tees, County Durham

6) James I
   Charles I
   Charles II
   James II
   Mary II
   Anne
7) Buxton, Derbyshire
   Alston, Cumberland
8) Edinburgh (St Giles Cathedral)
   Glasgow (Tolbooth Steeple)
   Aberdeen (King's College chapel)
9) Wakefield, Yorkshire
   St Ives, Huntingdonshire
   Bradford-on-Avon, Wiltshire
   Rotherham, Yorkshire
10) Brechin, Angus
    Abernethy, Perthshire

Page 21 – Associations – Counties

1) Cumberland
2) Bedfordshire
3) Cornwall
4) Pembrokeshire
5) Yorkshire
6) Cheshire
7) Fife
8) Huntingdonshire
9) Shropshire
10) Sussex

Page 22 – Associations – Towns And Cities

1) Bristol, Gloucestershire
2) Oxford, Oxfordshire
3) Paisley, Renfrewshire
4) Norwich, Norfolk
5) Plymouth, Devon
6) Reading, Berkshire
7) Dundee, Angus
8) Manchester, Lancashire
9) Swansea, Glamorgan
10) Cambridge, Cambridgeshire

Page 23 – Acronyms

1) Oscar Deutsch Entertains Our Nation
2) Driver and Vehicle Licensing Agency
3) Trevor
4) To Improve Performance
5) His Master's Voice
6) Morris Garages
7) Imperial Chemical Industries
8) Marylebone Cricket Club
9) British Broadcasting Corporation
10) Officer of the Order of the British Empire

Page 24 – Names

1) Florence Nightingale
2) Tudor (Ty Dur is Welsh for House of Steel)
3) Joseph Merrick
4) Kennedy
5) Billy Connolly
6) Dumfries
7) Windsor
8) Hellfire Club
9) John Bunyan
10) Edinburgh

Page 25 – Quotes

1) Charles I
2) Lord Nelson
3) Lloyd George
4) James Bond
5) Earl of Uxbridge (later Marquess of Anglesey) Duke of Wellington (at Battle of Waterloo)
6) Disraeli
7) G.K. Chesterton
8) Sherlock Holmes
9) Samuel Johnson
10) Nancy Astor Winston Churchill

Page 26 – Quotes

1) '. . . standing on the shoulders of giants' – Sir Isaac Newton
2) '. . . savaged by a dead sheep' – Denis Healey
3) '. . . entire of itself' – John Donne
4) '. . . makes a man healthy, wealthy and wise' – Benjamin Franklin
5) '. . . is of the weather' – Dr Johnson
6) '. . . more deadly than the male' – Rudyard Kipling
7) '. . . and that is not being talked about' – Oscar Wilde
8) '. . . where angels fear to tread' – Alexander Pope
9) '. . . when first we practice to deceive' – Sir Walter Scott
10) '. . . under some delusion' – Edmund Burke

Geography

Page 29

1) Ben Nevis 4409ft (1344m)
2) Mount Snowdon 3560ft (1085m)
3) Scafell Pike 3209 (978m)
4) Unst, Shetland
5) Dunnet Head, Caithness
6) Thurso, Caithness
7) Dee Estuary
8) Lowestoft Ness, Suffolk
9) Chepstow, Monmouthshire
10) Buchan Ness, Aberdeenshire

Page 30

1) Shetland
2) Jersey
3) Lizard Point, Cornwall
4) Mull of Galloway, Wigtownshire
5) Glamorgan
6) Mull of Galloway
7) Rockall
8) Argyllshire
9) Lands End, Cornwall
10) Gannet

Page 31

1) Cape Wrath
2) Lewis and Harris
3) Isle of Wight
4) Loch Lomond
5) Rutland Water
6) Bala Lake
7) Wastwater
8) Windermere
9) Pitlochry, Perthshire
10) Braemar, Aberdeenshire

Page 32

1) River Severn
2) River Tay
3) River Thames
4) Carmarthen
5) River Dee, Aberdeenshire
6) Cardigan Bay
7) Sutherland
8) Derbyshire
9) Cheddar Gorge, Somerset
10) Holme Fen, Huntingdonshire

Page 33

1) Yorkshire
2) Inverness-shire
3) Devon
4) Cardiff
5) Eastern Hemisphere
6) Aberdeen
   Dundee
   Edinburgh
   Glasgow
   Inverness
   Stirling
7) Wells, Somerset
8) Flash, Staffordshire 1518ft (463m)
9) Manchester
10) Norwich

History

1) Magna Carta
2) Battle of Edgehill, 23 October 1642 (Battle of Naseby 14 June 1645)
3) Alexander II
4) Ripon, Yorkshire
5) Charles I (at Dunfermline)
6) Dover Castle, Kent
7) John Knox
8) Edward, the Black Prince (Son of Edward III, he died in 1376, possibly of cancer, one year before his father)
9) Glenn Miller
10) Ruth Ellis

1) William I of Scotland (William the Lion)
2) York
3) Richard II
4) 1066
5) Fishguard, Pembrokeshire
6) HMS Victory
7) Mary I
8) Astronomer Royal
9) Denmark
10) St Davids

1) Duke of Monmouth
2) Stirling
3) Canterbury
4) France
5) Robin Hood
6) Milford Haven
7) 25
8) Catherine Parr
9) Leicester
10) Ireland

1) Queen Victoria (63 years, 7 months)
2) George II (Battle of Dettingen, 1743)
3) George VI (until 1949)
4) Elizabeth II (on 20 December 2007 she surpassed the 81 years and 243 days of Queen Victoria)
5) George V
6) William IV
7) Edward VIII (abdicated in December 1936)
8) Charles I (5ft 4ins)
9) Victoria
10) William III

Page 41

11) Edward the Confessor
12) Edward V
13) Edward III
14) Stephen
15) Henry VI
16) Henry I
17) Edward I
18) James II
19) William II (Rufus)
20) Richard III

Page 42

1) Malcolm III
2) James V
3) Donald III (Ban, or the Fair)
4) Kenneth I (Macalpin)
5) David II
6) James I
7) John (Balliol)
8) Mary, Queen Of Scots
9) James II
10) Alexander III

Page 43

1) Sir Alec Douglas-Home
2) The Earl of Bute
3) Tony Blair (Fettes)
4) Willam Gladstone
5) Lord Palmerston
6) Sir Robert Walpole (20

years 314 days)
7) Harold Macmillan
8) Harold Wilson
9) Viscount Melbourne
10) The Earl of Rosebery

Page 44

1) Margaret Thatcher
2) The Duke of Wellington
3) Tony Blair
4) Clement Attlee
5) Sir Robert Peel
6) Harold Macmillan
7) William Gladstone
8) Gordon Brown
9) James Callaghan
10) Margaret Thatcher

Page 45

1) Spencer Perceval
2) Arthur Balfour
3) David Lloyd George
4) The Duke of Wellington
5) Henry Campbell-Bannerman
6) William Gladstone
7) Winston Churchill
8) Ramsay MacDonald
9) Tony Blair
10) Andrew Bonar Law (born in New Brunswick, Canada)

Page 46

1) Lord Kitchener
2) Lord Birkenhead
3) Lloyd George
4) Sir Stafford Cripps
5) Dorothy Parker
6) Clement Attlee
7) Sir Stafford Cripps
8) Field Marshal Montgomery
9) Stanley Baldwin
10) Aneurin Bevan

Page 47

1) Tony Blair
2) Neville Chamberlain
3) James Callaghan
4) Edward Heath (on joining the Common Market)
5) Norman Tebbit
6) Margaret Thatcher (about her Deputy Willie Whitelaw)
7) Gordon Brown
8) Tony Blair
9) Harold Macmillan
10) John Major

Sport & Culture

Page 51- Sport

1) Cheltenham Race Course
2) Fred Perry
   Bonus: 3 – in 1934, 1935 and 1936
3) Two thousand guineas (Newmarket in April/May)
   One thousand guineas (Newmarket in early May)
   The Oaks (Epsom in early June)

The Derby (Epsom, first Saturday in June)
The St Leger (Doncaster in September)

4) Sam Torrance
5) Marquess of Queensberry
6) Glasgow Celtic
7) Katherine Jenkins
8) Lester Piggott

Page 52

9) Brooklands, Surrey
10) Michael Owen (18 years and 59 Days)
Bonus: Stanley Matthews (42 years 103 days)
11) Ipswich
12) Ayr
13) Donald Campbell
14) Cardiff
15) Lawn Tennis
16) Llanelli (the Scarlets)
17) Aintree
18) Tony Jacklin

Page 53

19) Chariots of Fire
20) Gary Lineker
21) Glasgow Celtic
22) Monty Panesar
23) Andy Murray
24) The Derby (in 1895 by Birt Acres)
25) Trevor Francis
26) Jim Clark
27) Gloucestershire
28) Graham and Damon Hill
29) Lottery
30) Edinburgh (Scotland v England 1871)
31) Sir Henry Cotton

Page 54

32) Tracy Edwards
33) Sunderland (USA 1894)
34) Mike Hawthorn (1958)
35) Jenny Pitman
Bonus: Corbiere 1983
36) Matthew Webb
37) Prestwick, Ayrshire
Bonus: 1860
38) Dr Roger Bannister
39) Andy Beattie
40) Malcolm Campbell

Page 55 – Food And Drink

1) Pineapple
2) Worcestershire Sauce
3) Swede
4) Liquorice
5) Self-raising flour
6) Wrexham, Denbighshire
7) Haig
8) Champagne
9) Pringles (see *I Never Knew That About The Scottish*, Roxburghshire)
10) Burton-On-Trent (utilising the yeast by-product from the brewing)

Page 56 – Music

1) International Music
   Eisteddfod
2) Felix Mendelssohn
   (Hebrides Overture)
3) Reading Abbey
4) Charlotte Church
5) The National Anthem
6) Virgin
7) Talking Heads
8) Posh Spice (Victoria
   Beckham)
9) Harry Lauder
10) John Barry

Page 57 – Entertainment

1) Brief Encounter
2) Michael Douglas (to
   Catherine Zeta-Jones)
3) Lord Profumo
4) Stewart Grainger
5) Oddjob
6) Port Talbot
7) Greer Garson
8) Under Milk Wood
9) Chitty Chitty Bang Bang
10) Maigret

Page 58 – Entertainment

1) Flint
2) Lyme Regis
3) Tenterden
4) The Railway Children
5) Shakespeare in Love
6) Peterborough
   Bonus: Catherine of Aragon
7) *Women in Love*
   A Touch of Class
8) Ealing Comedies
9) The Prisoner
   Bonus: questions: Patrick
   McGoohan and Danger
   Man
10) Pinewood Studios

Page 59 – Actors And Entertainers

1) Ben Kingsley
2) Baby Spice
3) Michael Caine
4) Stan Laurel (Laurel and
   Hardy)
5) Sting
6) David Tennant
7) Michael Crawford
8) Richard Burton
9) Boris Karloff
10) Ivor Novello

Page 60

1) Pre-Raphaelite
2) Scarborough, Yorkshire
   Bonus questions: Lord
   Leighton and Charles
   Laughton
3) Marlow, Buckinghamshire
4) Daniel Defoe
5) Mint cake
6) Ian Fleming
7) Roald Dahl
8) C.S. Lewis
9) William Gladstone
10) Robert Louis Stevenson

Page 61

1) Toad Hall
2) Henry Fielding
3) George Eliot
4) Somerset Maugham
5) Aphra Benn
   Bonus: Westminster Abbey
6) Hugh Lofting
7) *Lady Chatterley's Lover*
   Bonus: D.H. Lawrence
8) Horace Walpole
   Bonus: *The Castle of*
   Otranto
9) Dame Rebecca West
10) Mold, Flintshire

Page 62

1) St Trinians
2) Ophelia
3) *She*
   Bonus: Rider Haggard
4) *The Decline and Fall of the*
   Roman Empire
5) *The Pilgrim's Progress*
   Morte d'Arthur
   Fanny Hill
6) Thomas Gainsborough
7) Sir James Thornhill
   Bonus: William Hogarth
8) *Brewer's Dictionary of*
   Phrase and Fable
9) Jerome K. Jerome
10) *Rebecca*

Page 63

1) George Orwell
2) John le Carre
3) Joseph Conrad
4) Mary Wesley
5) Lewis Carroll
6) C.S. Forester
7) Anthony Burgess
8) Saki
9) Q
10) James Herriot

Page 64

1) Clive Staples
2) John Ronald Reuel
3) Joanne (Kathleen)
4) Pelham Grenville
5) Andrew Norman
6) Phyllis Dorothy
7) Edward Frederic
8) Thomas Edward
9) David Herbert
10) Herbert George

Page 65

1) Wilfred Owen
2) Laugharne
3) James Hogg
4) Grantchester, Cambridgeshire
   Bonus: Jeffrey Archer
5) The Earl of Aberdeen
6) Weeping Willow
7) A mouse
8) Aloysius
9) The Quantocks
10) Pistyll Rhaeadr, Denbighshire

Page 66

1) '. . . That is for ever England' – Rupert Brooke
2) '. . . as we that are left grow old' – Laurence Binyon
3) '. . . We have no time to stand and stare' – W.H. Davies
4) '. . . A stately pleasure dome decree' – Samuel Taylor Coleridge
5) '. . . deserves the fair' – John Dryden
6) '. . . homeward plods his weary way' – Thomas Gray
7) '. . . A host of golden daffodils' – William Wordsworth
8) '. . . bloody, but unbowed' – W.E. Henley
9) '. . . in the close tonight' – Sir Henry Newbolt
10) '. . . Let me count the ways' – Elizabeth Barrett Browning

First and Seconds

1) Redruth, Cornwall
2) Florence Nightingale
3) Thomas Cook
   Bonus: A temperance
   meeting in Loughborough
4) Stockton-On-Tees,
   County Durham
5) Joseph Fry
6) Peak District National
   Park
7) Dame Nellie Melba (Peach
   Melba)
8) Electric light bulb
9) Richard Arkwright

10) St Augustine
11) Railway accident
12) St Andrews
13) Henry III
    Bonus: French and Latin
14) Kenneth Tynan
15) William Bass
16) Henry Campbell-
    Bannerman
17) Walsall, Staffordshire
    Bonus: Nurse Dora
    Pattison (Erected 1886)
18) Australia
19) The Vyne

20) Louise Brown
21) Domesday Book
22) Brighton, Sussex
23) Penny Black
24) Matthew Boulton
25) Talbot
    Bonus: Alton Towers
26) *Casino Royale*
27) Wilton House, Wiltshire
28) Whitby Abbey, Yorkshire
29) John Logie Baird

30) Gordon
31) Gower Peninsular
32) Lossiemouth, Morayshire
33) How Much is That Doggie
    in the Window?
34) Derby
35) Durham
36) Charles Rolls
    Bonus: Charles Rolls
37) River Tyne

Page 77

81) Norfolk (Caister)
82) St Columba
83) Neil Kinnock
84) Inverary Castle
85) The tank
86) Orkney
87) William Caxton
88) Book Club
89) American War of Independence
90) Thomas Cranmer
     Bonus: Cardinal Reginald Pole

Page 78 – On second thoughts . . .

1) Hay-on-Wye, Breconshire
2) Norwich Cathedral (315 ft 96m)
3) Elgin
4) Glasgow
5) Alnwick, Northumberland

Page 79

6) Houghton Hall
7) Birmingham
8) Sir Nick Faldo
9) Rochester
10) Cambridge

Page 80 – And ultimately . . .

1) Derby
2) Linlithgow, West Lothian
3) Tewkesbury, Gloucestershire
4) The Honours of Scotland (they date from the early 16th century and were first used at the coronation of the infant Mary, Queen of Scots in 1543)
5) Dover Castle

Page 81

6) Yorkshire Terrier
7) Famous Grouse
8) Stafford
9) Conwy, Caernarfonshire
10) Eaton Hall, Cheshire
     Bonus: The Duke of Westminster

Buildings of Britain

1) Lincoln Cathedral
2) Kirkwall, Orkney
3) Winchester Cathedral
4) St Asaph, Flintshire
5) Southwell Minster (the 'Leaves' are carvings around the door to the Chapter House)

6) Oxford Cathedral
7) St Mungo
8) Bangor, Caernarfonshire
9) Dunblane Cathedral, Perthshire
10) St Albans Cathedral, Hertfordshire

11) Gloucester Cathedral
12) Dornoch Cathedral, Sutherland
13) Brecon Cathedral
14) Peterborough Cathedral
15) Aberdeen (St Machars)

1) Northamptonshire
2) (Elihu) Yale
3) Kendal, Wetmorland
4) Northamptonshire
5) Perth (the town's football club, St Johnstone, takes its name from St John's church)

6) St Mary Redcliffe, Bristol
7) Denbigh
8) A lance
9) Essex
10) Rutland Water

1) Framlingham, Suffolk
2) John Brown
3) Colchester
4) Constantinople
5) Catherine of Aragon

6) Drum Castle
7) Caerphilly Castle
8) Dover Castle
9) Dunbarton Castle
10) Conwy Castle

There's No Place Like Home

11) The Bronte Sisters
12) Lord Byron
13) T.E. Lawrence (Lawrence of Arabia)
14) Robert Maxwell
15) Morgan Family

16) John Milton
17) Agatha Christie
18) Nancy Astor
19) Thomas More
20) William Morris

Matchbox

Page 105 – Cathedral Matchbox 1

Answer – Liverpool Cathedral (is the largest Anglican cathedral in the world)
1) Canterbury has the oldest Norman crypt in the world
2) Exeter has the longest stretch of unbroken gothic vaulting in the world
3) Westminster has the widest nave in England
4) Durham was described by Sir Walter Scott as 'Half church of God, half castle 'gainst the Scot'

Page 106 – Cathedral Matchbox 2

Answer – Coventry Cathedral (houses Britain's tallest tapestry, 'Christ in Glory' by Graham Sutherland)
1) Llandaff houses 'Christ in Majesty', by Jacob Epstein

2) St Pauls is Britain's only domed cathedral
3) Ely is called the 'Ship of the Fens'
4) Wells has a mighty scissors arch inside

Page 107 – Inventions Matchbox 1

Answer – Richard Trevithick – (invented 3 – the steam locomotive)
1) The tractor was invented by Daniel Albone
2) The lawn mower was invented by Edwin Budding
4) The steam engine was invented by Thomas Newcomen
5) The seed drill was invented by Jethro Tull

Page 108 – Inventions Matchbox 2

Answer – John Harrison –
(invented 1 – the marine chronometer)

2) The television was invented by John Logie Baird
3) The steam boat was invented by William Symington
4) The jet was invented by Sir Frank Whittle
5) The stocking frame was invented by Revd William Lee

Page 109 – Matchbox Of Burial Places

Answer – Worcester Cathedral
(burial place of King John)

1) Stoke Poges is the burial place of Thomas Gray
2) Iona is the burial place of John Smith
3) St Enedoc's, Cornwall is the burial place of John Betjeman
4) Gloucester Cathedral is the burial place of Edward II

Counties of Britain

Page 113 – Aberdeenshire

1) Walt Disney
2) Gardenia
3) Queen Victoria
4) Guillotine
5) Marischal College

Page 114 – Anglesey

1) Thomas Telford
2) Anglesey
3) Tudors
4) Barbarella
5) Dawn French (one half of French and Saunders and married to Lenny Henry)

Page 115 – Angus

1) Stone of Scone
2) Unicorn
3) Princess Margaret
4) Adhesive postage stamp
5) Battle of Killiecrankie

Page 116 – Argyllshire

1) It is the westernmost point on mainland Britain
2) Loch Fyne
3) Campbeltown
4) Glencoe
5) Para Handy
   Bonus: Neil Munro

Page 117 – Ayrshire

1) Brig O' Doon
2) Johnny Walker
3) Ayr
4) Prestwick
   Royal Troon
   Turnberry
5) President Eisenhower

Page 118 – Banffshire

1) Fish Soup
2) Grants
3) Thomas Telford
4) Duff House, Banff
5) Tomintoul

Page 119 – Bedfordshire

1) John Howard
2) Watling Street
3) John Bunyan
4) Whitbreads (Samuel)
5) Shorts Brothers

Page 120 – Berkshire

1) William the Conqueror
2) The Merry Wives of
   Windsor
3) Reading
   Bonus: Henry I
4) *The Times*
5) Royal

Page 121 – Berwickshire

1) Silver
2) Earl Haig
3) Sir Walter Scott
4) Duns and Greenlaw –
   Duns won
5) River Tweed

Page 122 – Breconshire

1) Adelina Patti
2) Rorke's Drift
3) Usk
4) Eric Gill
5) Sarah Siddons

Page 123 – Buckinghamshire

1) Philadelphia
2) The Cock and The Bull
3) The Enigma Code
4) W.H. Smith
5) The Chiltern Hundreds

Page 124 – Buteshire

1) Prince Charles
2) Goat Fell
3) The Hamiltons
4) Millport, Great Cumbrae
5) Edmund Kean

Page 125 – Caernarfonshire

1) Conwy
2) Bardsey Island
3) Plaid Cymru
4) T.E.Lawrence (Lawrence of Arabia)
5) Llandudno

Page 126 – Caithness

1) Sinclair
2) The Pentland Firth
3) Castle of Mey
4) Monte Carlo Rally
5) The Boys Brigade

Page 127 – Cambridgeshire

1) 14th century
2) DNA
3) Yellow
4) Mary I (Tudor)
5) Great Clock of Westminster (Big Ben)

Page 128 – Cardiganshire

1) The Holy Grail
2) River Severn and River Wye
3) Llyn Brianne
4) Daffyd, the only gay in the village
5) Camera Obscura

Page 129 – Carmarthenshire

1) Dylan Thomas
2) The Scarlets
3) Lord Nelson
4) Pendine Sands
5) Gold

Page 130 – Cheshire

1) Birkenhead
2) Hollyoaks
3) River Weaver
4) Pemberley
5) George Mallory

Page 131 – Clackmannanshire

1) James VI of Scotland
2) Robert the Bruce ('Mannan' is a glove and 'Clach' is a stone)
3) Shipping
4) Nova Scotia
5) Ochil Hills

Page 132 – Cornwall

1) Furry Dance
2) *The Shell Seekers*
3) Minack Theatre
4) Torrey Canyon
5) Falmouth

Page 133 – Cumberland

1) The National Trust
2) Windscale
3) Whitehaven
4) John Peel
5) Alfred Wainwright

Page 134 – Denbighshire

1) Chirk Castle
2) Henry Morton Stanley
3) Pontcysyllte
4) Timothy Dalton
5) Prince Madoc

Page 135 – Derbyshire

1) Kinder Scout
2) Chatsworth
3) Barbara Castle
4) Herbert Spencer
5) River Derwent

Page 136 – Devon

1) Jack Russell
2) 1620
3) *Hound of The Baskervilles*
4) Abide With Me
5) Axminster

Page 137 – Dorset

1) Raleigh was smoking and the servant thought he was on fire
2) Tolpuddle Martyrs
3) Boy Scout movement
   Bonus: Robert Baden-Powell
4) Portland Stone
5) Hovis bread

Page 138 – Dumfriesshire

1) Edward I
2) Darien Scheme
3) Moffat
4) Robert Burns
5) Sanquhar

Page 139 – Dunbartonshire

1) Charles Rennie Mackintosh
2) Antonine Wall
3) Argyll
4) Luss
5) MacGregors

Page 140 – Durham

1) St Cuthbert
2) The Venerable Bede
3) A monkey
4) High Force
5) Washington (Gertrude Bell and Bryan Ferry were born there)

Page 141 – East Lothian

1) John Rennie
2) John Muir
3) Bass Rock
4) Samuel Smiles
5) The Battle of Prestonpans

Page 142 – Essex

1) Electricity
2) Castle Hedingham
3) Tiptree
4) Christopher Jones
5) Chelmsford

Page 143 – Fife

1) RAF Culross
2) The Royal and Ancient Golf Club (of St Andrews)
3) Dunfermline
4) Adam Smith and Robert Adam
5) James V

Page 144 – Flintshire

1) Rhuddlan
2) George III
3) St Winefride's
4) The first Welsh language bible
5) John Prescott

Page 145 – Glamorgan

1) Cremated
2) Pontypridd
3) William Randolph Hearst
4) Orangery
5) The Mumbles ('Mamelles')

Page 146 – Gloucestershire

1) William Tyndale
2) Alexander Selkirk
3) Double Gloucester
4) Sunday School
5) Matthew

Page 147 – Hampshire

1) Basingstoke
2) Charles I
3) Mother's Union
4) Charles Dickens
5) John Stonehouse
   Bonus: Sheila Buckley

Page 148 – The Hebrides

1) Islay (Bowmore)
2) Flora Macdonald (Betty Burke was Bonnie Prince Charlie in disguise)
3) George Orwell
4) Lewis
5) Isle of Skye

Page 149 – Herefordshire

1) Man of Ross
2) River Wye
3) Mappa Mundi
4) William Langland
5) Chained library

Page 150 – Hertfordshire

1) A Zeppelin
2) The Wicked Lady
3) Lady Caroline Lamb
4) A witch
5) A canal

Page 151 – Huntingdonshire

1) Oliver Cromwell
2) Henry Royce
3) Launcelot
4) Catherine of Aragon
5) T.S. Eliot

Page 152 – Inverness-shire

1) Monarch of the Glen
2) Gavin Maxwell
3) Culloden
4) Duncan Grant
5) The Green Beret

Page 153 – Kent

1) St Augustine
2) Augustus Pugin
3) River Medway
4) Saltwood Castle
5) Speeding

Page 154 – Kincardineshire

1) John Bull
2) Pneumatic tyre
3) Oliver Cromwell
4) A Gladstone bag
5) Japan

Page 155 – Kinross-shire

1) Loch Leven Castle
2) River Devon
3) T in the Park
4) William Adam
5) Mary, Queen of Scots

Page 156 – Kirkcudbrightshire

1) Balliol
2) River Nith
3) Merrick
4) John Paul Jones
5) James Clerk Maxwell

Page 157 – Lanarkshire

1) Hamilton
2) Lighthouses
3) Echo
4) Trongate
5) Glasgow Tower

Page 158 – Lancashire

1) (Sir) Loin of beef
2) Fly across the Atlantic
3) The Liver building
4) Spinning Jenny
   Spinning Mule
   Bonus: James Hargreaves
   Samuel Crompton
5) Pendle Hill

Page 159 – Leicestershire

1) Loughborough
2) The Secret Diary of Adrian Mole
3) Duke of Rutland
4) Cardinal Wolsey
5) Melton Mowbray

Page 160 – Lincolnshire

1) River Witham
2) Fish fingers
3) Methodist Church
4) Alfred Lord Tennyson
5) Louth

Page 161 – Merioneth

1) *Blithe Spirit*
2) Bala Lake
3) Lancastrians
4) It was the first possession ever given to the National Trust
5) Patagonia

Page 162 – Middlesex

1) The two minute silence
5) The postal service
3) William Hogarth
4) Horace Walpole
   Bonus: Strawberry Hill
5) The Black Hole of Calcutta

Page 163 – Midlothian

1) Encyclopaedia Britannica
2) James VI of Scotland
3) St Giles Cathedral
4) Logarithms
5) Rosslyn Chapel

Page 164 – Monmouthshire

1) Wordsworth
2) River Usk
3) Caerleon
4) Japanning
5) National Health Service

Page 165 – Montgomeryshire

1) Clive of India
2) Machynlleth
3) Llandiloes
4) Lloyds
5) Florence Nightingale

Page 166 – Morayshire

1) The Elgin Marbles
2) Elgin
3) Fochabers
4) Forres
5) Findhorn

Page 167 – Nairnshire

1) William McGonagall
2) Holly Tree
3) Calder
4) Capercaillie
5) Margaret Thatcher's

Page 168 – Norfolk

1) George Vancouver
2) Princess Diana
3) Burnham Thorpe
4) The ears (the Norfolk has dropped ears while the Norwich has pricked)
5) A bowler hat

Page 169 – Northamptonshire

1) Sir Thomas Tresham
2) Peterborough Cathedral
3) Nicholas Hawksmoor
   Bonus: Lord Hesketh Easton Neston
4) Radar
5) Lord Kitchener

Page 170 – Northumberland

1) Bamburgh Castle
2) St Aidan
3) Charles Parsons
4) Chillingham
5) Jackie and Bobby Charlton

Page 171 – Nottinghamshire

1) Little John
2) Boots
3) William Brewster
4) He was burned at the stake
5) Gotham

Page 172 – Orkney

1) Skara Brae
2) St Magnus
3) Italians
4) James III
5) Washington Irving

Page 173 – Oxfordshire

1) Lewis Carroll
2) Chaucer's
3) Latimer
   Ridley
   Cranmer
4) Isis
5) The Ashmolean Museum

Page 174 – Peeblesshire

1) The Duke of Queensberry
2) Chambers Dictionary
   (William and Robert
   Chambers)
3) Traquair House
4) Herbert Henry Asquith
5) *The Thirty Nine Steps*

Page 175 – Pembrokeshire

1) Equals sign =
2) Stonehenge
3) Wogan
4) Beavers
5) The Duke of Monmouth

Page 176 – Perthshire

1) Dunkeld
2) Blair Castle
3) Earthquakes
4) The Palace of Scone
5) Denis Lawson and Ewan
   McGregor

Page 177 – Radnorshire

1) Revd Francis Kilvert's
   diary
2) St Stephen
3) James Watt
4) Percy Bysshe Shelley
5) Offa's Dyke

Page 178 – Renfrewshire

1) James Watt
2) Ronald Reagan
3) The Stewarts
4) Rudolph Hess
5) Air Ambulance Service

Page 179 – Ross & Cromarty

1) Glenmorangie
2) Fulham (Mohammed
   Fayed)
3) Language
4) Camp Coffee
5) Gruinard

Page 180 – Roxburghshire

1) Robert the Bruce's
2) Skulls
3) Roxburgh
4) It spirals the opposite way
   to normal – for left handers
5) Sir Chay Blythe

Page 181 – Rutland

1) Horseshoes
2) Manners
3) Yellow
4) Titus Oates
5) Uppingham

Page 182 – Selkirkshire

1) Sir Walter Scott
2) Monmouth
3) Tweed
4) Mungo Park
5) A type of fruit loaf

Page 183 – Shetland

1) Whalsay
2) Dundas
3) Lerwick
4) P & O (Peninsula and Orient)
5) Norman Lamont

Page 184 – Shropshire

1) Charles Darwin
2) The Royal Oak
3) Bridgnorth
4) Thomas Parr
5) Much Wenlock

Page 185 – Somerset

1) Lorna Doone
2) Joseph of Arimathea
3) Bath Oliver
4) Wells
5) The Sweet Track

Page 186 – Staffordshire

1) Titanic
2) River Dove
3) Josiah Spode
4) The American Declaration of Independence
5) Heresy

Page 187 – Stirlingshire

1) Mary Livingstone
2) John Knox
3) The Battle of Stirling Bridge
4) The Carron Ironworks
5) River Nile

Page 188 – Suffolk

1) John Constable
2) Edward Fitzgerald
3) River Orwell
4) Newmarket
5) Rum

Page 189 – Surrey

1) Woking
2) Laurence Olivier
3) Actress Ellen Terry
4) Wandsworth
5) Multiplication sign ×

Page 190 – Sussex

1) National Velvet
2) King Canute
3) Henry Holland
   John Nash
4) Sir William Hamilton
   Bonus: Nelson
5) Hubert Parry

Page 191 – Sutherland

1) The Duke of Sutherland
2) The Hong Kong and
   Shanghai Banking
   Company – now HSBC
3) Andrew Carnegie
4) Mackay Clan
5) Smoo Cave

Page 192 – Warwickshire

1) The Mulberry Tree
2) The Lunar Society
3) Joseph Hansom
4) Lady Godiva
   Coventry
5) Meriden

Page 193 – West Lothian

1) Primrose
2) The Forth Railway Bridge
3) Tam Dalyell
4) Linlithgow
5) Abercorn

Page 194 – Westmorland

1) Taxes
2) Helvellyn
3) Topiary
4) Windermere
5) Catherine Parr

Page 195 – Wigtownshire

1) St Ninian
2) Gin
3) Wigtown
4) Gavin Maxwell
5) The Wicker Man

Page 196 – Wiltshire

1) Isambard Kingdom Brunel
2) Oxygen
3) To be eaten by a tiger
4) Lacock Abbey
5) Ian Fleming

Page 197 – Worcestershire

1) Peter Roget
2) Edward Elgar
3) *Brideshead Revisited*
4) Priest Holes
5) Morgan

Page 198 – Yorkshire

1) River Swale
2) Scarborough
3) Mackintosh's Toffee
4) Guy Fawkes
5) Holmfirth